37

★★★ PLAYERS IN ★★★

PINSTRIPES

Edited by Mark Vancil and Mark Mandrake

RARE AIR BOOKS

Created and Produced by Rare Air Books
A division of Rare Air Media
www.rareairmedia.com

A Ballantine Book
Published by Random House Publishing Group

www.ballantinebooks.com

The Library of Congress Cataloging in Publication Data is available upon request.

ISBN 0-345-48104-6

Manufactured in the United Kingdom

First Edition: November 2004

9 8 7 6 5 4 3 2 1

ACKNOWLEDGMENTS

At a moment's notice came an immediate response. What more could be asked of partners, particularly those with multiple responsibilities and limited time? Nothing actually, but that didn't stop anyone connected with this book from lending extra time, insight, talent and kindness to a process already squeezed by narrow schedules and unreasonable demands.

Then again, that's how Major League Baseball's Don Hintze has become the best in his business and why Mark Mandrake exemplifies the passion and commitment that drives the Yankees. We wouldn't have had a chance without their innate goodness.

At Rare Air Media, Nick DeCarlo never wavered in his pursuit of excellence even in the hours leading up to his wedding engagement, and Ken Leiker once again answered a call that came at the last minute without a second thought.

And thanks to the professionalism and insight of Anthony Ziccardi, Bill Takes, Jennifer Osborne and Gina Centrello. All publishing experiences should be this fulfilling.

Thanks one and all including, and not in the least, Laurita, Alexandra, Samantha, Isabella and Jonah. You remain the best of me.

Mark Vancil – 2004

To George M. Steinbrenner III, without whom stories of Yankees greatness would be much less great: For a winning tradition the Boss helped restore to sports' most successful team, as well as for the support he has shown me personally and professionally — sincere thanks.

Ever-tolerant Mark Vancil further reinforced his reputation as master juggler and delightful business partner.

Of the Yankee Stadium front office, Al Santasiere, Ken Derry and Glenn Slavin were indispensable on this project. Long nights, early mornings and nonexistent weekends rewarded the continued subjugation of self-interests for this trio. Michael Margolis' editorial alacrity was amazing. Lonn Trost always found a way to squeeze publishing dilemmas into an impossible calendar. Lou Rocco didn't let the photography awards go to his head and grabbed the best shots in the face of adversity.

The interior of this book would have been hollow without cooperation of the ballplayers, managers, and coaches — most particularly Joe Torre, Reggie Jackson, Whitey Ford, Don Mattingly, Goose Gossage, Willie Randolph, Derek Jeter, Paul O'Neill, and Bobby Murcer — whose insights and narrative skills shaped many of these pages. Yogi Berra and Phil Rizzuto lent us not only their collaboration, but that of their grandchildren: Gretchen Berra, Lindsay Berra and Jennifer Rizzuto Congregane.

It's tough to summarize in a few sentences the continued patience shown by my family through the bedlam of recent years. With a Mandrakean (not to mention Yankees-like) flair for high drama, my beautiful daughter Violet Veronica entered the world at the conclusion of the deciding game of the 2003 World Series. Since that day, Violet has proved a blessing to my productivity and the highest inspiration to completing assignments. Heartfelt appreciation also goes to Hanley, Melissa, Janet, and particularly to Jackie — still my wife and my life.

SPECIAL THANKS

W.C. Burdick, Brad Horn, Jeff Idelson, and Scot Mondore at the National Baseball Hall of Fame and Museum; Heather Benz, Bob Bowman, Patrick Courtney, Paul Cunningham, Mark Feinsand, Phyllis Merhige, Rich Pilling, and Lindsay Reid at Major League Baseball; former and current Yankees staff Kristen Aiken, Doug Behar, Brian Cashman, Joe Flannino, Howard Grosswirth, Jeff Jackson, Jerry Laveroni, Andra McCartney, Arthur Richman, Jayna Rust, Neil Schwartz, Frank Swaine, Michael Tusiani, and Deborah Tymon; other baseball officials Dick Bresciani, Larry Cancro, Barry Gossage, Steve Green, Marty Greenspun, Michael Huang, Marc Levine, Debbie Matson, Kim Ng, Bernadette Repko, and John SooHoo; Dave Kaplan of the Yogi Berra Museum; Larry Burke and Mark Mravic of Sports Illustrated; empirical thanks to Harris Atkins, Eugenie Bisulco, Jeff Botwinick, John Camilleri, Jaime Collins, Larry Desautels, Minna Edelman, Jackie Feinberg, Dr. Charles V. Hamilton, Jamie Herskowitz, Michael Kinstlinger, Marc Miller, Steve Moscov, Bernie Nuñez, Matt Perachi, Michael Shabsels, Patrice St. John, Robert St. John and Alan Ziegler for their support, advice and friendship.

Mark Mandrake – 2004

PHOTOGRAPHY

Photography except as noted below copyright © Corbis Bettman Archives and Mark Mandrake, Lou Rocco, Bernie Nuñez/New York Yankees

Photographer	Pages	Photographer	Pages
John Dominis/TimePix	88, 92	Peter Read Miller/Sports Illustrated	66-67
Bob Gomel/TimePix	98	Ralph Morse/TimePix	25, 96, 104
Walter Iooss Jr.	2-3, 38, 40, 56, 58, 59, 71, 72, 75	Hy Peskin/TimePix	52
Mark Kauffman/TimePix	50	Ezra Shaw/Getty Images	118
National Baseball Hall of Fame Library, Cooperstown, NY	63	John G. Zimmerman/TimePix	99

12
20

TABLE *of* CONTENTS

NYSE
adidas
DODGE
Armitron
OAKLAND
YANKEES

★★★ FROM ★★★

BABE RUTH TO ALEX RODRIGUEZ

ANOTHER TRADE OF THE CENTURY DEFINES THE YANKEES

Players come and players go, and in the history of sports, only a few player trades have resonated through the industry as loudly as the February 2004 exchange that sent Alex Rodriguez from the Texas Rangers to the Yankees.

And in baseball, the last trade that involved such an accomplished player in his prime — without the shadow of free agency — might have been the one that sent Babe Ruth from Boston to the Yankees, and changed the history of both franchises.

As did the Rodriguez deal.

In the case of Rodriguez, the cost to the Yankees was substantial: Alfonso Soriano, who had been hitting home runs and stealing bases at a greater rate than any other major league second baseman, and almost half of the record $252 million contract that Rodriguez had signed three years earlier.

A player of Rodriguez's caliber — many regarded him as the game's best player — had not changed teams in a trade since the Seattle Mariners sent Ken Griffey Jr. to the Cincinnati Reds prior to the 2000 season. The Griffey deal was influenced by his pending free-agent status; Rodriguez had seven years remaining on his contract. Otherwise, there had been only one other player traded in the last 40 years who at the time of the deal might have been considered the equal of Rodriguez. Jose Canseco went from the Oakland Athletics to the Rangers in 1992, a year after he hit 44 home runs, drove in 122 runs, scored 115 runs and stole 26 bases.

Still, it's likely that not even the Ruth deal cre-

move to the Bronx. The deal created such a stir that even the President of the United States issued a statement.

"I was just as surprised as the Yankee fans and the Boston Red Sox fans when I opened up my paper today," said George W. Bush, who once owned the Rangers. "It obviously is a big deal. A-Rod's a great player and the Yanks are going to be a heck of a team with him in the infield."

Others weighed in with an opinion, too:

✦ **FORMER NEW YORK CITY MAYOR RUDOLPH GIULIANI**, a longtime Yankees fan, relished the thought of A-Rod and Derek Jeter playing side by side: "It's great for the city. He's returning home. [Rodriguez was born in New York City, but grew up in Miami, Florida.] This could be another variation of Maris-Mantle, Jackson-Munson, Gehrig-Ruth."

✦ **FORMER YANKEES STAR REGGIE JACKSON**: "This is a fabulous move for the Yankees. It is good for baseball and good for Rodriguez. He needs to compete against history, against the lineage of the game's greatest players."

✦ **YANKEES OWNER GEORGE STEINBRENNER**: "I'm pretty excited. This is a big, big one. It ranks with when

Rodriguez became the first player ever traded who had been his league's Most Valuable Player the previous season. For eight years, Rodriguez had been making his case for being the best shortstop in the history of the game. He had the top two home run–hitting seasons ever by a shortstop, and the fourth-best RBI total ever at his position. He became the first infielder — and just the third player — to hit 40 home runs and steal 40 bases in the same season. By the end of the 2003 season, Rodriguez was set to shatter Cal Ripken's home run record for shortstops — at the age of 27. He was a .340 hitter in postseason games. He won a batting championship, and twice was awarded a Gold Glove for fielding excellence. And if that wasn't enough, Rodriguez signed the $252 million contract, by far the richest ever for a professional athlete, prior to the 2001 season.

But for all of Rodriguez's personal glory, he never got close to the World Series with either the Mariners or the Rangers. Seattle was competitive, making the playoffs three times, but Rodriguez couldn't budge the Rangers out of last place in any of his three years with the team.

There were at least two other twists that made the trade as big and loud as any that had come before. The fact that Texas very publicly had tried to trade Rodriguez to the Boston Red Sox in December 2003 only made his eventual arrival in New York juicier for the Big Apple faithful.

For a while, it looked like Rodriguez would remain in Texas, and Aaron Boone, the hero of the 2003 League Championship Series, would remain at third base for the Yankees.

Then the game changed. Boone went down with a knee injury, and Rodriguez was back in play with one more twist. If he landed with the Yankees, where would he play? Rodriguez had won a Gold Glove at shortstop in 2003, but Derek Jeter, the leader and captain of the Yankees, occupied that position in the Bronx.

Rodriguez never wavered.

"It's Derek's team," he said. By any measure other than World Series championship rings, Jeter was a lesser player than Rodriguez. But those rings suggest more than any numbers could, even in a game defined by numbers. And in Jeter's case, the rings define the intangibles that define greatness.

"There are things that go beyond ability," says Yankees manager Joe Torre. "There's something special about Derek Jeter, who doesn't hit 20 home runs, doesn't knock in 100 runs, doesn't steal 30 bases. It's something that you can't put down on paper, and that's my job to have a feel for that."

So Rodriguez cheerfully moved to third base. At 28, he still had time to set his credentials as the greatest third baseman in baseball history.

"I've come to a point in my career when winning is the most important thing," Rodriguez said. "And being a New York Yankee provides the opportunity. When you drive to the ballpark, every day you have a chance to win.

"I told Derek, 'I'm going to stick close to you, ask your advice on many issues. I need your support and mentorship.' Derek has four world championships, and I want him to have 10. That's what this is all about."

Rodriguez and the Yankees were a union made for Major League Baseball's marketing department. A clean-living and exemplary leader, Rodriguez now wore the pinstriped uniform of the world's most famous sports team. Not only is he talented, handsome, famous and wealthy, but also charismatic, humble, respectful and gracious. A telling moment about Rodriguez came at the 2001 All-Star Game. He had been selected as the American League's starting shortstop, and Cal Ripken Jr. as the starter at third. But just before the game started, Rodriguez insisted Ripken, who was in his final season, switch positions. So Ripken moved to shortstop, the position he had become famous for, and Rodriguez was able to honor a baseball icon while playing alongside his boyhood hero.

Though expectations for Rodriguez and the Yankees are enormous, none of them seem unreasonable. A-Rod is expected to become the Yankees first right-handed hitter to reach 40 home runs in a season since Joe DiMaggio hit 46 in 1937. And the Yankees, assuming they get Jason Giambi back healthy, could become the greatest home run machine of all time.

Then there are the Red Sox. In 2004, Rodriguez started off at .200 with only one home run and three RBI in the first four series with Boston, in which the Red Sox won 8 of 13 games. Yet it was in one of those games that Rodriguez earned a place in Yankees–Red Sox lore. After being struck by a pitch from Bronson Arroyo, Rodriguez was front-and-center in a full-scale brawl, adding another chapter to a rich and intense rivalry between the two teams.

A-Rod had arrived in pinstripes, just like Ruth before him. Now all A-Rod needed was a championship ring to complete the outfit.

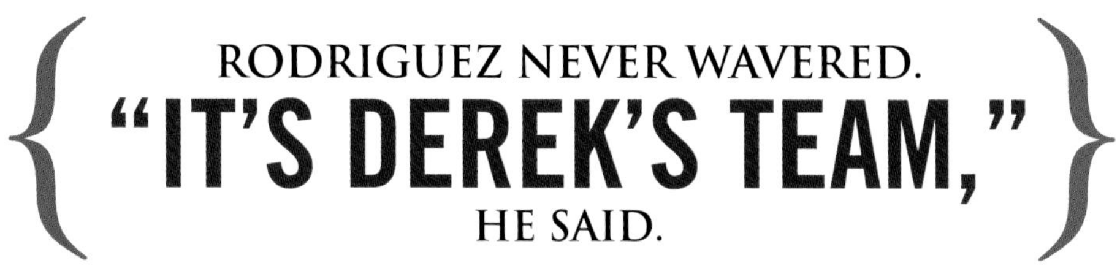

PLAYERS *in* PINSTRIPES

BABE RUTH'S ENDURING LEGACY

— Essay by Robert W. Creamer

AN ALL-TIME YANKEES TEAM

Selected by the New York–New Jersey Chapter of the Baseball Writers Association of America

Babe Ruth was the first New York Yankees player to go from baseball fame to American legend, but he wasn't the last. From Ruth, Gehrig, DiMaggio and Mantle to Jackson and Jeter, there always has been something unique about those wearing Yankee pinstripes. It is within this context that award-winning author Robert W. Creamer examines in the following essay the enduring relevance of Ruth. Also, we dissect the 25-man all-time Yankees team, as it was voted by the New York–New Jersey Chapter of the Baseball Writers Association of America, and analyze other great players, some of whom were lost in the shadows of their more famous teammates.

NY
AL LEADER IN
ON BASE % 10 TIMES
RBI 6 TIMES
WALKS 11 TIMES
SLUGGING % 13 TIMES
HR 12 TIMES
RUNS 8 TIMES
Sultan of Swat

BABE RUTH'S ENDURING LEGACY

Essay by Robert W. Creamer

Babe Ruth has not swung a bat at a pitch in a major league game since 1935, and he has been dead for more than 50 years. And still we talk about him. How come? His storied record of 60 home runs in a season was broken more than 40 years ago. The lingering glamour of the "Babe's 60" has been trampled and all but obliterated by sluggers racing toward and beyond that once magical mark.

Ruth's career record of 714 homers was surpassed a generation ago. His incredible slugging average for one season "xxx", a record that lasted 80 years, is gone. His near-legendary number of walks in one season "xxx", most of them intentional or nearly so, has been topped. When the Babe retired, he held 56 major league records, but that majestic castle of achievement is crumbling.

And still we talk about him. In 1973, 25 years after Ruth's death, the columnist Red Smith wrote that the Babe seemed "insistently alive," and after 30 more years it continues to be that way. "Babe Ruth" seems to jump into print and discussions almost every day. Why is he recalled so vividly? What was it about Ruth — what *is* it about him — that keeps him so alive?

The answer is *impact.* Ruth made an impact on everyone who saw him, from his schoolboy days at St. Mary's Industrial School for Boys in Baltimore to his final burst of three home runs in one game in Pittsburgh, a few days before his playing career ended. He simply dominated the scene wherever he was, on and off the field, with his size (at 6-feet-2-inches and 235 pounds, he was a very large person for his day), his big round face, his booming voice, his infectious, outgoing personality, his extravagant behavior, the dramatic scope of his accomplishments on the ballfield, the way he changed baseball and perhaps, beyond everything else, the way he created the image of the New York Yankees that continues to this day.

Ruth made the Yankees. Before he went from Boston to New York, in January 1920, the Yankees were nothing. The now glamorous team name was only seven years old when the Babe arrived — New York's American League club had been called the "Highlanders" for 10 seasons before that. From the club's inception in 1903 through 1919, it had never won a pennant, had finished second only twice, and in most seasons was a drab, mediocre team. Some years it was worse than mediocre. The encyclopedic *Total Baseball* claims that in 1913 the new manager, Frank Chance, inherited "the weakest lineup the New York Yankees will ever have." The Yankees had been last in 1912. Under Chance they edged up to seventh in 1913, one game above last place, and in 1914 they climbed into a tie for sixth place.

Jacob Ruppert and Cap Huston bought the club after the 1914 season, and things began to improve, if slowly. Ruppert and Huston, men about town in Manhattan, had looked into buying John McGraw's New York Giants, at the time baseball's most famous team. McGraw turned them away, so they bought the Yankees, who in 1913 had abandoned their old hilltop stadium to play in the big, modern Polo Grounds as the Giants' tenants. The Yanks finished fourth in 1918 and third in 1919, but they were still considered a second-rate team.

Then Ruth arrived, and the baseball world changed. One must appreciate the situation. Ruth had come into the big leagues as a left-handed pitcher, and he proved to be a great one. In his first full season, in 1915, he won 18 games. He followed that with 23 victories in 1916 and 24 in 1917. He had 13 wins in 1918 in a war-shortened season during which he also played the outfield much of the time. As a pitcher, he won three games without a loss in World Series competition, including a 14-inning, 2-1 masterpiece in 1916 that was the longest World Series game played in the 20th Century. He pitched 29 consecutive scoreless innings in Series play, breaking the great Christy Mathewson's record set 13 years earlier. Ruth's record lasted for 43 years.

Ruth was one hell of a pitcher, but that wasn't all he was in those days. During his first three seasons as a pitcher, Ruth hit nine home runs — four in 1915, three in 1916 and two in 1917. Even today that many homers by a pitcher might attract attention. Back then, in the dead-ball era, it was sensational.

The American League home run leader in 1915 was an outfielder named Braggo Roth, who played for Chicago and Cleveland and hit seven home runs; three more than Ruth, four more than Ty Cobb and two more than Shoeless Joe Jackson. The National League leader was Gavvy Cravath, who hit 24.

And here was a 20-year-old rookie, a pitcher, with four home runs in 1915. Beyond that astonishing development was the way Ruth hit them, the power he displayed. Ruth's first major league homer, hit in May 1915 in the Polo Grounds where his Red Sox were playing the Yankees, landed in the upper right field stands; a gargantuan poke in that era and particularly impressive because, as an awed sportswriter pointed out, the young pitcher hit it "with no apparent effort."

"As soon as I got out there I felt a strange relationship with the pitcher's mound. It just felt like the most natural thing in the world. Striking out batters was easy."

— BABE RUTH

Ruth hit another home run in the Polo Grounds a month later, prompting another journalist to intone: "His name is Babe Ruth. He is built like a bale of cotton and pitches left-handed for the Boston Red Sox. All left-handers are peculiar and Babe is no exception, because he can also bat."

He hit his third homer that season into the distant right field bleachers in Boston's Fenway Park, where only one ball had ever been hit previously, and his fourth sailed completely out of Sportsman's Park in St. Louis, breaking a plateglass window on the far side of the street. In that game in St. Louis, Ruth also had two doubles and a single, drove in three runs, and pitched a complete game in a 4-3 victory.

Ruth hit only three homers in 1916. They came in successive games, noteworthy anytime but amazing in 1916, particularly because one of them was a pinch-hit, three-run, game-tying blast. Of his two home runs in 1917, one was the first ever hit into the center field seats at Fenway Park. The other was something of a command performance: He was pitching in New York, in front of a crowd largely made up of newly inducted soldiers (this was during World War I) who had been brought to the ballpark as a farewell treat before shipping out. The soldiers wanted to see Ruth hit one. The Babe, who loved interacting with the crowd, tried to accommodate them. He brought them to their feet with a roar in the sixth inning when he drove a long "foul home run" over the right field roof before settling for a single. When he came to bat in the ninth inning, the soldiers beseeching him to belt one, he came

"When you figure the things he did, and the way he lived and the way he played, you've got to figure he was more than an animal even. There was never anyone like him. He was a god."

– **JOE DUGAN, Ruth's teammate, 1922–1928**

through, hitting his second and last homer of the year.

By that time, even though Ruth had hit only nine home runs in his career, he was being called "The Home Run King." In spring training of 1918, the Red Sox stopped at an Army camp to play an exhibition game, and Ruth put on a show in batting practice, knocking five balls over the right field fence. People just didn't hit a ball that far that frequently in those days, and for the assembled soldiers it was like watching a sudden explosion of skyrockets. Cheers of delight erupted every time a ball sailed beyond the distant fence.

That was the season Ruth began playing the outfield when he wasn't pitching, and he tied for the American League home run title with 11. In 1919, as Ruth completed the transition from full-time pitcher to full-time hitter — he started 15 games on the mound and won nine — he hit 29 homers, two more than the previous major league record. He was just 24, yet he had become the most compelling figure in the game. "The more I see of Babe," said the respected Boston sportswriter Burt Whitman, "the more he seems a figure out of mythology."

And at that point Ruth was sold to the Yankees.

Think of the impact. The Yankees were improving, but in a city dominated by McGraw and the Giants, who had finished first or second 13 times in 17 years, the Yankees still were nothing. Far more people went to the Polo Grounds to see the Giants play than to see the Yankees. Now, suddenly, stunningly, the lowly Yankees had Babe Ruth, the game's best and most popular player — and Ruth came through for them far beyond their wildest dreams.

He started slowly in the 1920 season, as though for dramatic effect. Opening Day was in

> "I saw him transformed into the idol of American youth and the symbol of baseball the world over, a man loved by more people and with an intensity of feeling that perhaps has never been equaled before or since. I saw a man transformed into something pretty close to a god."
>
> — **HARRY HOOPER**, **Ruth's teammate, 1914–1919**

Philadelphia. The Yankees' regular center fielder had been injured, and Ruth persuaded manager Miller Huggins to let him play that position. He hit two singles, but also dropped a fly ball in the eighth inning with two outs and two on. The homer-less spell persisted in Philadelphia and then in Boston, where the Yankees lost three games to the Red Sox before returning to New York for the home opener. A big crowd turned out that afternoon, but Ruth's New York debut was a fizzle. He suffered a pulled rib cage muscle during batting practice, struck out in the first inning, and was taken out of the game, a great disappointment for the fans. Ruth didn't play again in that greatly anticipated weekend series, and in the first game upon his return he struck out twice and made an error.

Some were murmuring: "How good is this Babe Ruth?" The "Ruthless Red Sox," as sportswriters had begun to call the Boston team, were leading the league, and the Yankees, with Ruth, were in the second division. Boston came to New York for a five-game series and won the first game, the fourth straight time the Red Sox had beaten the Yankees in the young season.

As the calendar turned to May, Ruth began to deliver. On the first day of the month, he hit his first home run of the season, and the Yankees beat the Sox. By the end of May, he had struck 12 home runs; far more than any other major leaguer had ever hit in one month, and as many as any other American League player, other than the Babe, had hit in a full season since 1903.

He hit a dozen in June. He mounted a 26-game hitting streak, even though he was walked intentionally game after game. His batting average climbed into the .390s before settling at .376 by the

"I swing as hard as I can and I try to swing right through the ball. The harder you grip the bat, the more you can s wing through the ball and the farther the ball will go. I swing big, with everything I've got. I hit big or miss big. I like to live as big as I can."

— BABE RUTH

end of the season. Ruth passed his 1919 home run record in the middle of July and finished the season with an utterly astonishing 54 homers, 35 ahead of the second man, George Sisler, who himself hit a remarkable 19. The Yankees were in the middle of the pennant race for a change, and in the end they finished third — a game short of second and three games behind the first-place Cleveland Indians.

Spectators poured into the Polo Grounds to see Ruth, many of them fans new to the game, drawn by the siren call of the Babe's explosive hitting. Season attendance at major league ballparks in the early decades of the 20th Century was much less than it is now. In the post–World War I glow of 1919, the year before Ruth joined the team, the Yankees had set a club record by drawing 619,000 spectators to the Polo Grounds, 24 percent more than their previous high. In 1920, with Ruth, they drew 1,289,000. Not only was it the first time a major league team had drawn a million in a season, but it was also 42 percent better than the previous record, set a dozen years earlier by McGraw's Giants.

Ruth's impact on baseball in 1920 was far greater than any player's previously or since. Beyond the record number of home runs and the record attendance for which he was largely responsible, he changed the way major league baseball was played. Whether the owners had altered the baseball from "dead" to "lively" is still debated, but there is no doubt they made changes with the intent of benefiting the hitters. They banned trick pitches such as the spitball and the emeryball, and they ended the long-standing practice of letting scuffed, dirty balls remain in play. Other players rushed to copy Ruth's swing-for-the-seats style. As home run totals began to soar, managers shifted their strategic approach from the traditional bunt-steal-sacrifice mode of creating runs to the long ball. Even McGraw, high priest of "old-school" baseball, followed along, despite the

Babe Ruth, Miller Huggins and Lou Gehrig during spring training in 1929.

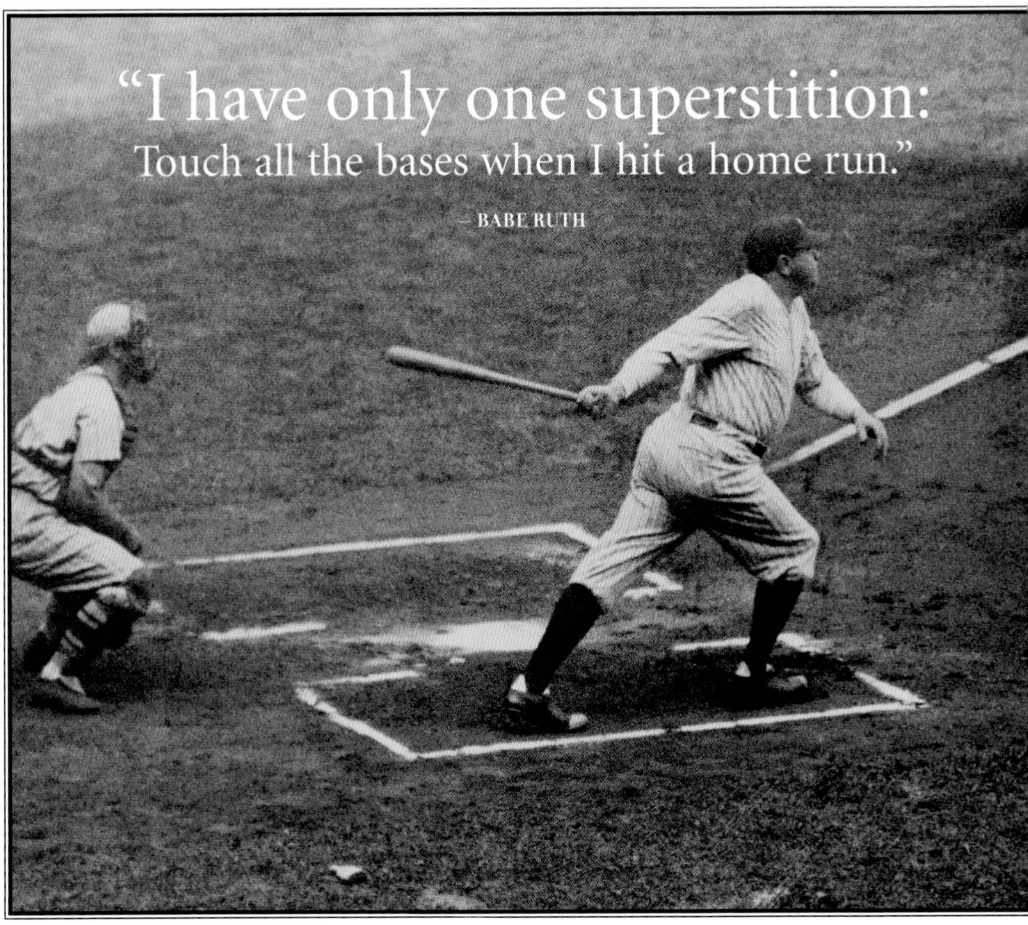

disparaging comments he made about Ruth and his style of hitting. Casey Stengel, who played three seasons for the Giants, said, "McGraw was the best manager I ever saw at adapting from the dead ball to the lively ball."

Ruth's performance in 1920 shook baseball at its moorings, and nothing was ever quite the same again. Even the Chicago Black Sox scandal, the shocking revelation late in the 1920 season that eight players on the 1919 White Sox had been paid to intentionally lose the World Series, was little more than a blip on the baseball screen. Attendance dipped briefly, then soared in the Roaring '20s, Ruth's big decade. Fans jammed into ballparks, enticed in good part by the home run efflorescence.

Ruth's popularity was enormous. Hank Greenberg, who a decade and a half later became a renowned home run hitter, said that when he was growing up in the Bronx, Ruth was the hero of every boy in the neighborhood. Harry Hooper, who had been a teammate of Ruth's in Boston, said, "I saw him transformed into the idol of American youth and the symbol of baseball the world over, a man loved by more people and with an intensity of feeling that perhaps has never been equaled before or since. I saw a man transformed into something pretty close to a god."

Throughout the 1920s Ruth remained center stage, usually heroically but sometimes as the bad boy. He had an even better season in 1921 than he did in 1920, hitting 59 homers to break the home run record for the third year in a row and leading the Yankees to their first pennant. As the author

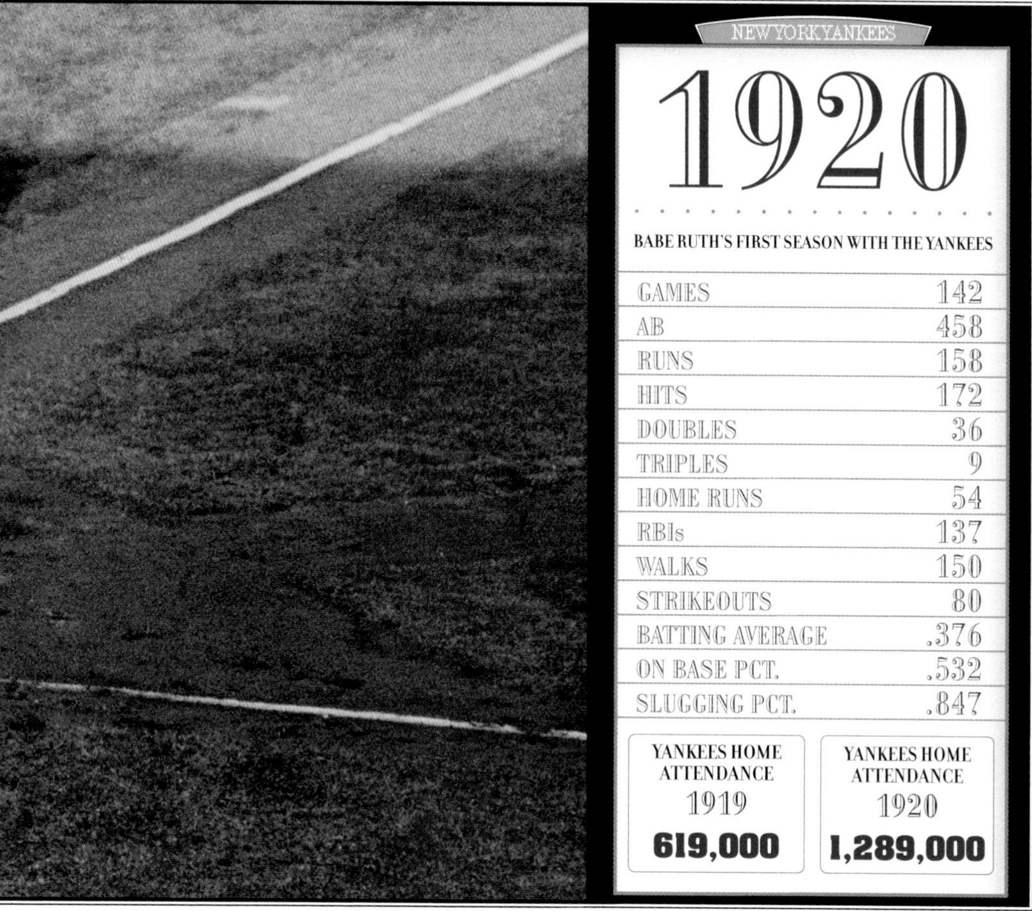
NEW YORK YANKEES

1920

BABE RUTH'S FIRST SEASON WITH THE YANKEES

GAMES	142
AB	458
RUNS	158
HITS	172
DOUBLES	36
TRIPLES	9
HOME RUNS	54
RBIs	137
WALKS	150
STRIKEOUTS	80
BATTING AVERAGE	.376
ON BASE PCT.	.532
SLUGGING PCT.	.847

YANKEES HOME ATTENDANCE 1919	YANKEES HOME ATTENDANCE 1920
619,000	**1,289,000**

Robert Lipsyte noted, "It is often overlooked that the home run king was probably the most complete player of his time — not only was he a superb major league pitcher, but his fielding and base-running were far above average too." Players who watched the left-handed Ruth fool around at third base during spring training in the 1920s marveled at his agility. The legendary New York sportswriter Red Smith said, "A person familiar with Ruth only through photographs and records could hardly be blamed for assuming that he was a blubbery freak whose ability to hit balls across county lines was all that kept him in the big leagues. The truth is that he was the complete ballplayer, certainly one of the greatest and maybe the best one of all time." The Yanks finished first again in 1922 and 1923, won the first of their many World Series championships in 1923, won three pennants in a row from 1926 through 1928 — six pennants in eight years was unprecedented success — and won World Series titles in 1927 and 1928.

Ruth was on a rollercoaster ride of both popularity and disapproval throughout those years. He was suspended by the baseball commissioner for the first six weeks of the 1922 season for his flagrant disregard of a rule that prohibited offseason barnstorming tours, and four more times that season, for shorter periods, as a result of his hot-tempered misbehavior. After he was ejected from a game for throwing dirt on an umpire, Ruth climbed over the dugout roof and charged into the stands after a heckler. In another game he ran in from the outfield to curse an umpire who had

"I never saw the Babe make a mistake in a ballgame. Ruth always knew, instinctively, what to do on a ballfield."

— ED BARROW, Yankees general manager, 1921–1945

called a play against the Yankees. He fought with a teammate in the dugout. People were both repelled and entranced. A contemporary observer, Paul Gallico, wrote, "There has always been a magic about that gross, ugly, coarse, gargantuan figure of a man and everything he did."

Ruth reformed and had great seasons in 1923 and 1924, but he got in serious trouble again in 1925. In spring training he was so involved with "booze and broads," as his friend and teammate Joe Dugan told me, that he developed an ulcer, collapsed, was hospitalized, underwent surgery on his abdomen and missed the first two months of the season. Upon his return, with his first marriage breaking up in a glare of publicity, Ruth played poorly, defied his manager, Miller Huggins, was suspended from the team, and fined the then-enormous sum of $5,000, an amount about equal to the yearly salary of most players at the time.

As a player Ruth reformed for good after that, but his eminently public private life — his extravagant appetite, his uninhibited manner of living, his separation from his wife, her death, his marriage to his second wife — fascinated people. Ruth's play on the field and his essentially good nature kept his popularity high despite the trouble he often found himself in. "There wasn't a mean bone in his body," said a teammate. Another added, "He was the kind of bad boy it's easy to forgive." Red Smith observed, "His natural liking for people communicated itself to the public."

Through it all, Ruth kept hitting home runs. Except for his two troubled seasons — 1922 and 1925 — he led the league in homers every year from 1918 through 1931, and he continued to hit them with a splendor and sense of dramatic timing that made them unforgettable. "There are a hundred stories illustrating his sense of theater," Smith said. Ruth hit the first home run in Yankee Stadium, on Opening Day in 1923, when that still-splendid ballpark was first opened to the public. He hit the first home run in the first All-Star Game. He set a home run record for the fourth time in 1927, out-dueling teammate Lou Gehrig and hitting 60. He hit three home runs in a World Series game in 1926 and again in 1928. Reggie Jackson is the only other player in the 20th Century that hit three homers in a Series game.

In the 1928 Series, St. Louis Cardinals fans hooted at Ruth as he stood in right field, and in turn he cheerfully pantomimed that he was going

"He was one of a kind. If he had never played ball, if you had never heard of him and passed him on Broadway, you'd turn around and look back."

— WAITE HOYT, Ruth's teammate, 1921–1930

to hit a homer his next time at bat — and he did. Ruth enjoyed doing extravagant things like that. In the late 1920s in Boston, he reacted to a box-seat fan loudly taunting him during a game in nearly empty Fenway Park by looking at the fan, pointing toward the right field seats, and hitting a ball there.

Ruth's most famous "called shot" came in Chicago in 1932 during a turbulent World Series between the Yankees and the Cubs. In the third game, with the score tied and the Cubs players and fans riding him unmercifully for a misplay he had made in the outfield, Ruth grinned, indicated he was going to hit a home run and sent a tremendous shot to dead center field — at that time the longest home run ever hit in Wrigley Field. Ruth's performance that day has been exaggerated, misinterpreted and distorted by Hollywood movies, television re-creations and misinformed commentary, all keyed to the question of whether he pointed to the exact spot where he intended to hit the ball and then hit it there. Almost certainly, Ruth didn't point to the exact spot in distant center field. What is significant is that in a World Series game in front of a huge, jeering crowd, he challenged Chicago and the Cubs, clearly implied he was going to smack one, and did smack one; not a cheap shot but a titanic homer that proved to be the game-winning run and the turning point of the Series. It was epic. Ruth, who relished such moments, loved it. He said later, "I never had so much fun in my life. That's the first time I ever got the players and the fans going at the same time."

Even as his career neared its end, Ruth created an unforgettable memory. In 1935, his last season, playing out the string with the Boston Braves, out of shape, aching, and making one last road trip before retiring, he somehow roused a final flash of his remarkable ability and hit three home runs in a game against the Pirates in Pittsburgh. The final homer, his 714th, the last hit of his career, was a colossal poke over the right field roof of towering Forbes Field, the first ball hit that far in Pittsburgh. Guy Bush, who was pitching for the Pirates, said later, "I never saw a ball hit so hard before or since. It's probably still going."

At that point no one except Ruth had hit 700 home runs, no one else had hit 600, no one had hit 500, no one had hit 400. Ruth had 350 more home runs than the man with the next biggest number, and 400 more than the man in third place. He was indeed the king of the home run.

Ruth's hold on the public hardly diminished after he left the stage in 1935. In the ensuing 13 years before his death from cancer at age 53, he continued to pop into the spotlight. When he went to Ebbets Field with his wife in 1938, to see the first night game played in Brooklyn, his presence created such a tremendous stir in the crowd that it was reported in New York newspapers the next day, along with what happened on the field that night: Johnny Vander Meer's second successive no-hitter. The publicity-conscious Dodgers soon convinced Ruth to be their first base coach for the rest of the season. Even then, potbellied and in his 40s, he put on a daily show for the fans, taking batting practice with the team and usually putting a ball or two over the fence. He would take infield practice too, at first base, where he displayed surprising grace for a man of his age and portly appearance, deftly scooping low throws out of the dirt.

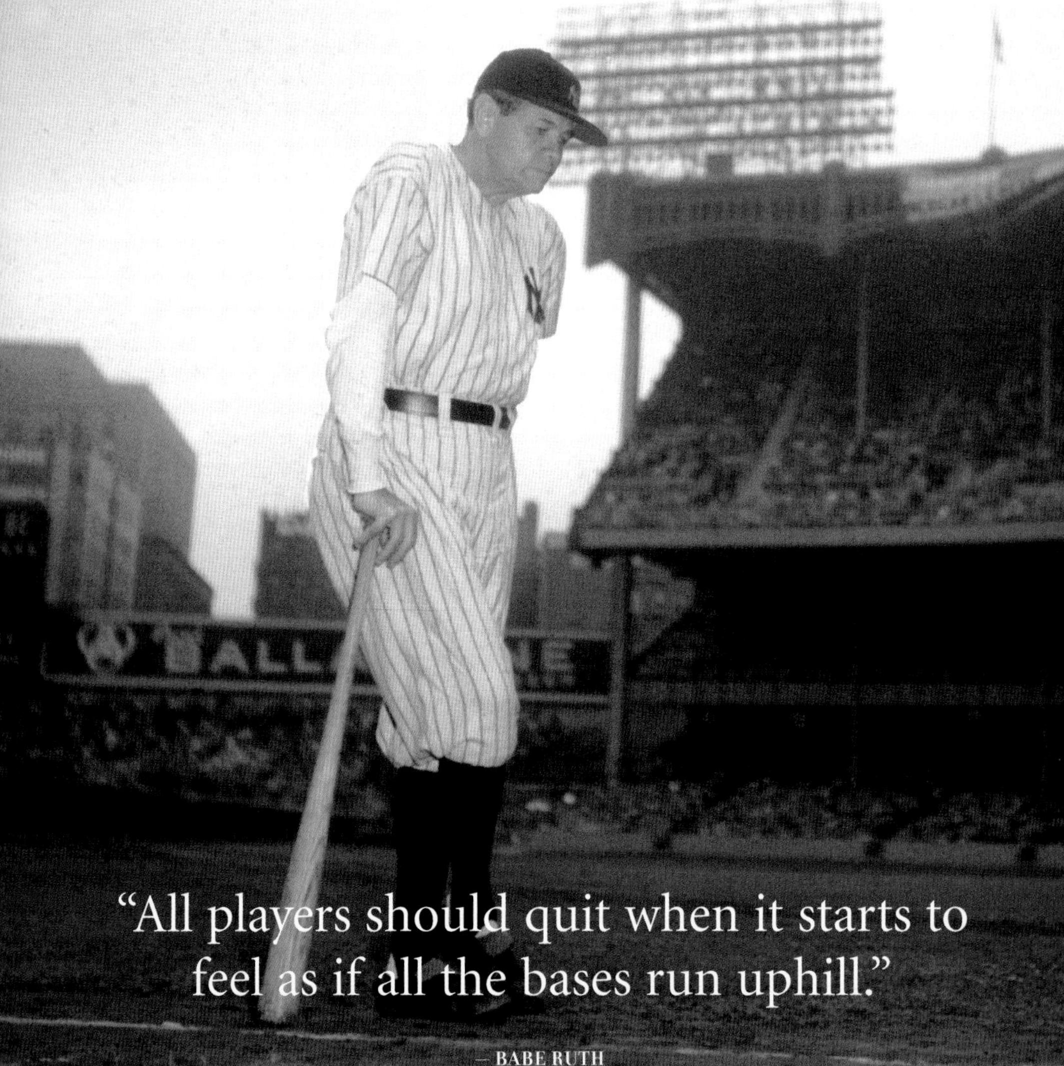

"All players should quit when it starts to feel as if all the bases run uphill."

— BABE RUTH

He remained a public figure, a notable, a celebrity. He was Babe Ruth. He was news during World War II when he batted against Walter Johnson or played golf with Ty Cobb in fund-raising events. He was in the public eye when he made an impressive motion picture appearance playing himself in the 1942 movie *Pride of the Yankees*, about his dead teammate Gehrig. Ruth's own death in 1948, after a long and painful illness, was very much a public event. There are elderly people today who remember where they were when they heard that Ruth had died, the way they remember where they were when they heard of Pearl Harbor or John F. Kennedy's assassination or September 11. Ruth's casket lay in state in the cavernous area under the stands in Yankee Stadium before his funeral mass at St. Patrick's Cathedral in New York, and an estimated 75,000 people passed it to pay their final respects. In pre-television America, when most major league ballplayers, most professional athletes, were seldom recognized in public, everyone knew Babe Ruth.

Crowds of mourners jammed the sidewalks on August 19, 1948, to watch the funeral procession for Babe Ruth as it moved toward St. Patrick's Cathedral in New York. Ruth's widow requested that the funeral service be open to anyone who wished to attend.

"He was one of a kind," said his teammate Waite Hoyt. "If he had never played ball, if you had never heard of him and passed him on Broadway, you'd turn around and look back." Ruth handled it all very well. He was naturally at ease in crowds, relished the acclaim and affection and reacted cheerfully. Simply put, he liked people and they loved him.

Ruth's towering presence didn't disappear with his death. Whenever a slugger began to hit homers at a rapid pace, a comparison inevitably was made between his growing total and the number Ruth had on the same date in 1927, his record home run season. In 1961, when Roger Maris and Mickey Mantle made their determined and successful (for Maris) assault on Ruth's 60 homers, Ruth was mentioned in print and on the air almost as often as Mantle and Maris were. A dozen years later, when Hank Aaron steadily approached and eventually surpassed Ruth's career home run total, the same thing happened. Aaron said in 1974, "I can't recall a day this year or last that I did not hear the name of Babe Ruth." Years after his death, the Babe was as alive in people's minds as Roger and Mickey and Hank were.

Ruth remained in mind for the rest of the 20th Century. When Ken Burns made his nine-part television documentary *Baseball* in 1994, one of the segments was devoted to Ruth. In 1995, on the 100th anniversary of the Babe's birth, Hofstra University on Long Island held a three-day seminar on the subject of Ruth. In 1998 the long-gone Babe was in the news again when Mark McGwire and Sammy Sosa engaged in their spirited home run duel in which both surpassed the records set by Ruth and Maris, and which ended with McGwire hitting 70 homers, a figure that seemed as magical as Ruth's 60 — except that it was to be surpassed three years later by Barry Bonds' 73.

In 1999, ESPN had a yearlong countdown on television of the 20th Century's "100 Greatest American Athletes," culminating in, so to speak, a competition between Ruth and Michael Jordan for the No. 1 spot. Jordan was the choice, although Ruth's adherents argued that the time bias was vastly in Michael's favor. Never mind. The old century ended and the new one began, and Ruth was still on people's minds. As Red Smith said, "There won't ever be a second Babe Ruth. Never another like him."

ALL-TIME YANKEES TEAM

Selected by the New York–New Jersey Chapters of the Baseball Writers Association of America

OUTFIELD

Joe DiMaggio
Reggie Jackson
Mickey Mantle
Babe Ruth
Roy White
Bernie Williams
Dave Winfield

INFIELD

Lou Gehrig
Derek Jeter
Tony Lazzeri
Don Mattingly
Graig Nettles
Willie Randolph
Phil Rizzuto

PITCHERS

Jack Chesbro
Whitey Ford
Lefty Gomez
Goose Gossage
Ron Guidry
Allie Reynolds
Mariano Rivera
Red Ruffing

Yogi Berra
Bill Dickey
Elston Howard

"I didn't think a guy could be that good. Every time I looked up, that big guy was on base or flying by me on a homer."

— CHARLIE GRIMM, Cubs first baseman, after Gehrig hit .529 in the 1932 World Series

Lou Gehrig

Let us suppose that the final, sad chapter of Lou Gehrig's career had not come about as it did, that his time in baseball had ended in a normal fashion. What would the last years of his career have been like?

There are no definitive answers to these questions. But one thing is quite apparent: Had he not been stopped by illness, Gehrig would have set major league career records for runs scored and RBI, and he would hold those records today by large margins. Babe Ruth held the career RBI record (2,213) and was passed only by Hank Aaron. Gehrig, despite losing out on possibly five years of his career, is fourth on the all-time list.

Comparing where they stood in RBI at age 35, Gehrig was 270 ahead of Aaron, and 280 ahead of Ruth. Gehrig turned 35 in 1938, and he began to fade in the second half of that season. His career ended in the first month of the 1939 season.

Until developing the disease that would later kill him, Gehrig raced ahead of Aaron and Ruth in RBI at a stunning pace. Aaron became a regular at age 20 and Gehrig at age 22, which afforded Aaron about a 200-RBI head start as they settled into their careers. At 28, Gehrig had 995, Aaron 991. At 30, Gehrig had 69 more than Aaron. At 32, Gehrig led by 137, and at 34 by 253. Gehrig pushed his advantage to 270 in 1938, even though, by his standards, it was a so-so season.

Aaron played until he was 42 and finished with 2,297 RBI. Gehrig was done at 35 and finished with 1,995. How high might Gehrig have taken that total?

The toughest part of answering that question is figuring out how long Gehrig would have played. If you would know that, you could pencil in the other numbers based on his career path and be satisfied with your projection. But you could miss by years guessing when Gehrig might have retired.

In good health, Gehrig certainly would have played every game in 1939, 1940 and 1941, at which time he would have been 38. Aside from poor health, it is difficult to fathom any reason why he would have left the lineup before 1942. By the end of the 1943 season, Gehrig might not have been playing every game, but almost certainly he would have still been playing. He would have been 40, and few stars of his magnitude retire before that age. Ruth, Aaron, Ty Cobb, Willie Mays, Honus Wagner, Stan Musial, Ted Williams, Tris Speaker — they all played at least until 40. Only a half-dozen true superstars in history retired before the age of 40, three of them Yankees (Gehrig, DiMaggio and Mantle).

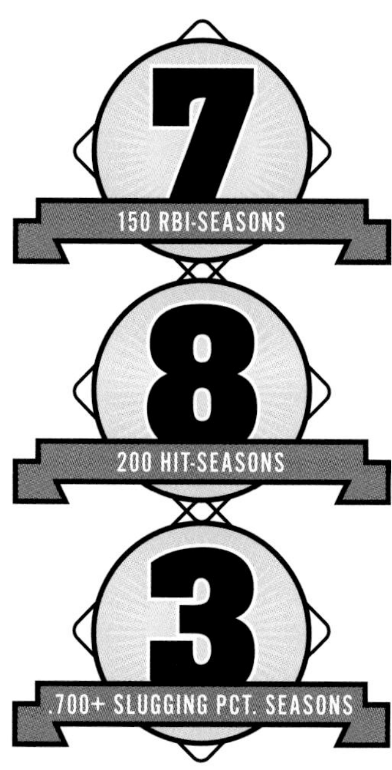

Now you come to a question that is impossible to answer: Would Gehrig have played through World War II? By 1943 the United States was in the thick of war, and great stars such as DiMaggio, Williams and Bob Feller were in military service. Gehrig probably was too old to be drafted into service. He could have volunteered, but few men of his age did. It is reasonable to assume that a healthy Gehrig would have been one of the best players in the American League in 1943 and would have continued playing through the war years, through 1945, when he would have been 42. Gehrig probably would not have been driving in 150 runs a season during the war years, for two reasons: He was getting older, and offensive statistics were dropping sharply before the war and during the war.

Gehrig's career batting average, frozen at .340, probably would have dropped to about .328. His home run total, based on conservative assumptions, would have approached 700 (it is 493). His RBI total would have been about 2,850 — approximately 550 more than the all-time record. That is a phenomenal total, but certainly within the realm of possibility, based on Gehrig's rate of achievement.

Gehrig would have set numerous other records that would remain today. He would have scored more than 2,700 runs — hundreds more than the existing record; he would have been just short of 4,000 hits; and he would have had about 7,150 total bases — 300 more than Aaron's all-time record. And Gehrig would have drawn almost 2,500 walks, again, hundreds more than the existing record.

As it is, Gehrig had 13 100-RBI seasons, a record he shares with Ruth and Jimmie Foxx, and 13 consecutive 100-RBI seasons, a record he shares with Foxx. It is safe to assume that Gehrig, in continued good health, would have had 17 or 18 100-RBI seasons.

What about his record for consecutive games played? He certainly could have extended it to 2,700 or 2,800. It likely would have reached 3,000. If that had been the case, Cal Ripken Jr. would not have broken Gehrig's record in 1995. Ripken would have had to play every day until early in the 2001 season to have passed Gehrig.

The fact is that Gehrig's name almost certainly would be throughout the major league record book for batting feats — and perhaps it would be the most prominent name in the book — had he not been struck down in his prime by the disease that now carries his name.

In a cold, logical analysis unpolluted by emotion, Babe Ruth remains the greatest baseball player the world has ever seen.

BABE RUTH

Funny thing about Babe Ruth: He's been dead and buried for more than half a century, yet he keeps having bad years. Roger Maris hit 61 home runs in 1961, breaking Ruth's season record of 60. The same year, pitcher Whitey Ford stretched his streak of scoreless innings in the World Series to 32, breaking a record Ruth had held since 1918.

In 1974, Henry Aaron broke one of Ruth's big records, number of home runs in a career, and others have picked off a few of Ruth's lesser records. In 2001, Rickey Henderson broke Ruth's record for career walks "since passed by Barry Bonds", and Bonds broke Ruth's records for walks, slugging percentage, and road home runs in a season.

Ruth is like a giant block of marble. Chip away and chip away, and what is left is a giant statue. Ruth lives on not only in the records he still holds, but in myth, in legend, and in the minds of the millions who grew up in the shadow of his memory.

In a cold, logical analysis unpolluted by emotion, Ruth remains the greatest baseball player the world has ever seen. Why? Because Ruth won more games for his team than anyone else has. Ruth hit .342 in his career, a tremendously impressive average — but Ty Cobb hit .367 and Rogers Hornsby .358; even Riggs Stephenson hit .336. Hitters do a lot of things other than hit singles. Cobb's batting average represents 60 percent of his value as a hitter, Hornsby's represents 55 percent of his batting value, and Stephenson's 59 percent. In Ruth's case, so many of his hits were home runs and he walked so often that his batting average represents only 38 percent of his offensive value. When you add to that Ruth's

achievement as a pitcher, he remains clearly the greatest player the game has ever had.

Why Ruth was the greatest player ever can be discussed on a different level. What made the man so special? The answer can be summed up succinctly: He had an enduring disrespect for rules. Ruth didn't acknowledge rules until he found from experience that they applied to him. It is a thread that ran throughout his life, and it goes a long way to explain why he was always ahead of the crowd.

A few years ago, a traveling baseball exhibit showcased one of Ruth's bats. Dave Henderson, a 1980s-era major league outfielder, studied the bat and discovered what everyone had missed for 60 years: The bat was corked. The end had been sawed off and glued back on. Any number of sportswriters assured us that Ruth never would have used a corked bat. Of course Ruth would have used a corked bat — unless someone stopped him. Indeed, the Babe was caught using an illegal bat in August 1922.

Ruth pushed and tested every rule and convention ever presented to him. Remember the story of when the President of the United States came onto the field to be introduced to the Yankees? They all held their caps in their hands and spoke respectfully to the President.

"How are you, Mr. President."

"Nice to meet you, sir."

"I'm honored to meet you, sir."

Then the President came to the Babe, who mopped his brow and remarked casually, "Hot as hell, ain't it, Prez?"

Remember the story about Ruth at a dinner party being offered asparagus? "No thanks, ma'am," he said politely. "It makes my urine stink."

Ruth knew the rules — he just tried to ignore the ones that cramped his style. Flouting the rules tied Ruth's life together, the major events as well as the minor anecdotes. As a child, he was sent to live in a supervised residence — St. Mary's Industrial School for Boys — because he refused to go to school.

Major League Baseball instituted a rule in 1911 prohibiting players on the World Series teams from touring on All-Star teams during the offseason. Commissioner Kenesaw Mountain Landis was adamant that the rule would be enforced, yet Ruth nonetheless organized an

All-Star team after the 1921 Series — and was suspended for the first six weeks of the 1922 season as punishment.

Have you heard of the "Bellyache Heard Round the World"? Ruth missed a third of the 1925 season allegedly because of abdominal distress caused by poor eating habits. The Babe long had laughed off warnings that his unhealthy diet was going to harm him.

Remember the story about Ruth dangling Miller Huggins, the diminutive Yankees manager, off the caboose of a moving train? Of course it was unacceptable behavior — but Ruth had a deep-seated dislike for authority figures.

Ruth's reluctance to accept rules without at least making an attempt to bend them is precisely what made him the hitter he was. When Ruth was in his teens, the men who taught baseball to youths virtually prohibited an uppercut swing. The old-school coaches taught that uppercutting, while it might afford a batter more distance when he connected and produce some home runs, would result mostly in fly-ball outs. Ruth ignored this. Some historians say he was allowed to swing with an uppercut because he was a pitcher, and no one took his hitting style seriously. They are dead wrong. Ruth swung contrary to the norm because it was not in his nature to do what he was told. In that way, Ruth was about as American as you can get. This is not a nation of obedient people who blindly respect leaders and convention. Americans like to push the envelope, see how far they can go.

Ruth did this better than most. Some of his challenges are to be admired; some are to be deplored. But there is no mistake that his refusal to swing a bat in the conventional manner of the times altered the course of baseball. He took the home run from a rarity to an omnipresent threat, and as a result the game's popularity soared.

.690	714	2,213
Ranks first all-time in slugging percentage	Ranks second all-time in home runs	Ranks second all-time in runs batted in

NY
R

REGGIE JACKSON

If you could go back and see the young Reggie Jackson the way a scout would see him, the first thing you'd notice would be Jackson's throwing arm. As a young man, Jackson could fire bullets from the warning track to third base. Of course he couldn't hit the broad side of a barn. But that was Reggie — he would get your attention.

Few players have ever had such an interesting combination of strengths and weaknesses as Jackson had. By the time he was 30, he had lost his powerful arm, but his skills remained a jumble of the spectacular. He could hit a baseball 500 feet, but he also led the league in strikeouts in each of his first four seasons, and over his career struck out 650 times more than any other player in major league history. He was fast as a young player and sometimes did clever things on the bases, but he wasn't a base-stealer or a consistently good base-runner. He never was close to leading the league in stolen bases, but he did lead once in times caught stealing.

Jackson led American League outfielders in errors as often as he did in strikeouts. His career fielding percentage compared to the league norm for outfielders (.967 versus .980) is among the worst in history. Many of his errors resulted from the same cause as the strikeouts: Reggie would try the impossible. He didn't mind failing when striving for the spectacular, a trait that all great performers share.

Because Jackson did some things stunningly well, many regarded him as a superstar. Because he struck out a lot, committed fielding errors and made mistakes on the bases, some did not regard him as a very good player. On October 18, 1977, Reggie won over a lot of his critics. That's the night he hit three home runs on three pitches in the sixth game of the World Series — after batting .353 with two home runs in the first five games. Jackson lived for the big stage and the chance to do something special, and he often did. In addition to his 1977 achievements, he also was the MVP of the 1973 Series.

As a player, Jackson was a lot like Sammy Sosa is. But Jackson didn't hit 60 homers a year, because, unlike Sosa, he didn't play in the funny-number era that began in the 1990s, and he didn't play half his games in Wrigley Field. The difference between Jackson and an average outfielder over the course of his career was 55 errors. What's 55 errors against 1,700 RBI? Same with Jackson's strikeouts. If a player has 2,597 strikeouts and 563 home runs, is he outstanding? Of course he is. If you take away the home runs and the strikeouts from Jackson, his career batting average is .301 and his on-base percentage is .424.

Statistical analysts do not warm to the idea of clutch hitters because they can't predict who will come through in a clutch situation. The guy who hits .450 in the clutch one year can just as well hit .150 the next. If it's not predictable, is it really a skill? It is one thing to say that it isn't a skill, but that's very different than denying that Jackson had many more than his share of dramatic, high-impact home runs, doubles and base-running credits.

Jackson doesn't need extra credit to prop him up as a star. He created runs; that's the bottom line for a hitter. Five hundred sixty-three home runs, 18 more homers in postseason play, five World Championship rings — the man came up big an awful lot. As for the rest of the Reggie package, any real baseball aficionado can live with it.

All-Time Team

RIGHT FIELD

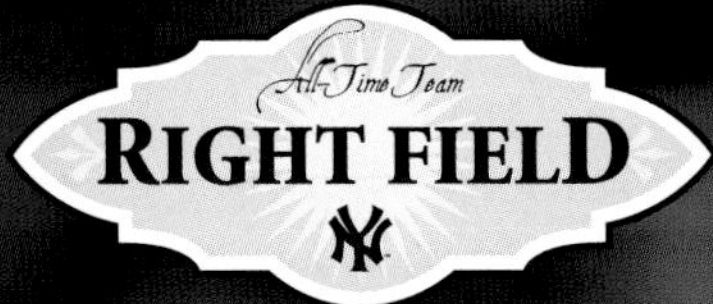

DAVE WINFIELD

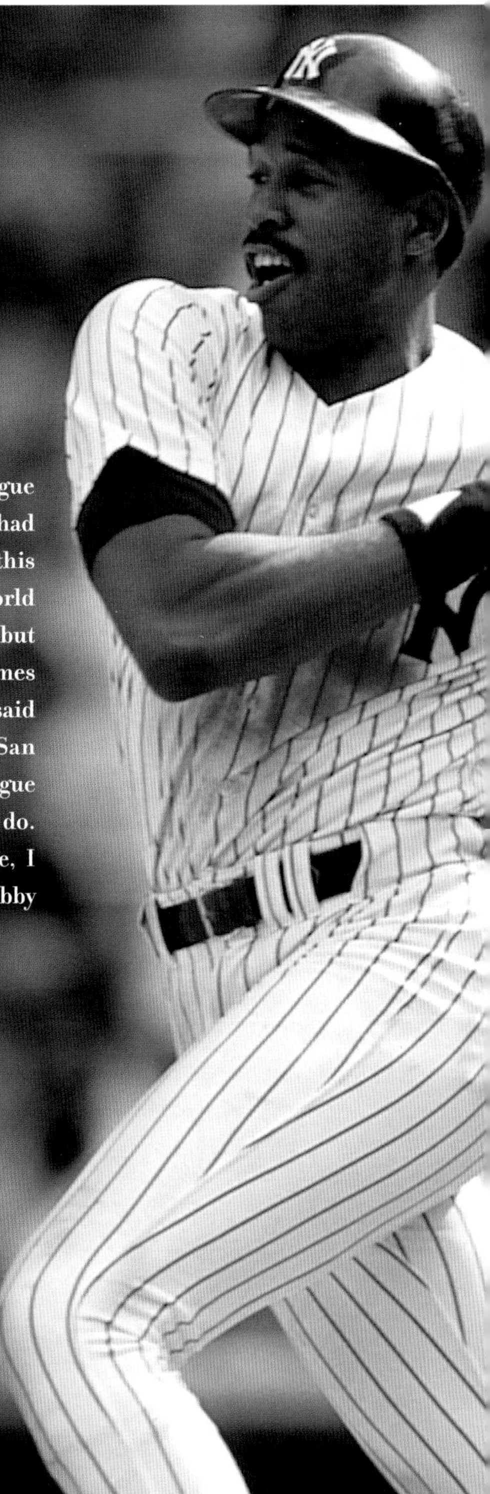

Throughout the 1970s, the American League fought the perception that the National League had more talent. There wasn't a good reason behind this misconception. The American League won the World Series in 1970, 1972, 1973, 1974, 1977 and 1978, but the National League won most of the All-Star games and seemed to have more stars. As Billy Martin said after the Yankees traded Bobby Murcer to San Francisco for Bobby Bonds: "The National League does a better job of promoting its stars than we do. When Bobby Bonds was in the National League, I thought he could walk on water. You know what? Bobby Murcer is a better player than Bobby Bonds."

In his eight full seasons with the Yankees, Winfield had 812 RBI. That's more than Eddie Murray, Mike Schmidt or anyone else in the major leagues had for that span.

Dave Winfield, after eight years with the San Diego Padres, joined the Yankees in 1981 with the reputation for being able to walk on water. Winfield almost certainly was the best player in the National League in 1979. He led the league in both total bases and RBI, despite playing for a terrible team in a pitcher's park. The Yankees in those days faced more left-handed pitchers than any other team, and the right-handed hitting Winfield was an ideal fit in the middle of their lineup, surrounded by left-handed power hitters.

Winfield led the Yankees in RBI in his first season, but he did not fare well in postseason play, going 10 for 55, including 1 for 22 in the 1981 World Series, when the Yankees lost to the Dodgers in six games. Reggie Jackson left the Yankees after that season, and Winfield was expected to replace Jackson's performance and presence. However, the Yankees never again got to the World Series with Winfield in their uniform, which he wore until early in the 1990 season.

The Yankees played a lot of good ball with Winfield in their lineup. They won 91 games in 1983, 97 in 1985 and 90 in 1986. During the 1980s, the Yankees had the best record in the major leagues. Yet the measure of success in the Bronx is the World Series, and the Yankees kept falling short. For that, Winfield received much of the blame. The man was a consistent run-producer, accounting for 116 RBI in 1983, 114 in 1985 and 107 in 1988, yet it never was quite enough to satisfy his critics. Winfield was judged by the standards of Jackson, Ruth, Mantle, DiMaggio — and he was expected to meet those standards with Butch Wynegar catching and Bobby Meacham playing shortstop. The challenge for Winfield was daunting, and it's a credit to him that he continued to excel.

In his eight full seasons with the Yankees, Winfield had 812 RBI. That's more than Eddie Murray, Mike Schmidt or anyone else had in the major leagues for that span. Winfield also was among the top 10 in the major leagues for those years in home runs, runs scored, hits and doubles. He won Gold Gloves because he was fast and had a powerful throwing arm, although those who watched him play every day saw a lot of balls drop safely in front of him.

Winfield was a tall, graceful and powerful athlete. He ran like the wind once he got his long legs in motion. He was the best athlete in baseball, in the sense that if you wanted a player who also could play basketball, football and track, he would have been the first man to choose. He was an athlete's athlete who had his choice of professional sports, and he selected baseball. Like the greatest Yankees who preceded him, Winfield is in the Hall of Fame, although he never is afforded as much acclaim as the others are, largely because the Yankees World Championship ledger shows a gap for the 1980s.

NY

YOGI BERRA

Everyone knows Yogi. How many athletes are famous enough to be featured in TV ad campaigns 40 years after they have retired? How many athletes are quoted regularly by the President of the United States?

Yogi was a short, funny-looking guy with knobby features who had a way of bollixing up the English language that would occasionally render the obvious profound. Come to think of it, that's still a description of Yogi.

He grew up in St. Louis at a time when the Cardinals signed all the good athletes in the area. They signed Yogi's boyhood pal, Joe Garagiola, to a bonus contract, but would not pay the same amount for Yogi because, well . . . *Does that man look like an athlete?* Garagiola, Yogi and their pals knew that Yogi was the best athlete in the group, but he just didn't look the part. Yogi wouldn't sign with the Cardinals for less than what Garagiola got, so instead he signed with the Yankees.

Bill Dickey "learned" Yogi all of his experience, as Yogi would say in one of his earliest Yogi-isms — and Yogi surpassed Dickey as the greatest catcher in Yankees history, perhaps even in baseball history. Whether Yogi was greater than Johnny Bench is a tough call. And whether Yogi was greater than Josh Gibson is impossible to know. But to claim that Dickey was better than Berra, frankly, is preposterous.

Dickey's career batting average was .313; Yogi's .285. Batting average is a useful and important statistic, but generations of fans have been inclined to draw too close a connection between a high batting average and a good player. If a high batting average always meant a good player, then a team with a high batting average would always win, and a team with a low batting average would always lose. A cursory look at the team batting average lists will show you that's not the way it is. A hitter's job isn't to compile a high batting average, but rather to create runs. If you focus on the "runs" categories rather than the batting average, Berra's advantages are apparent. He scored far more runs than Dickey (1,175 to 930) and drove in far more runs (1,430 to 1,209).

For every 162 games played, Dickey scored 84 runs and drove in 109; Berra scored 90 and drove in 109. The numbers are almost identical, but not the value. First, Dickey played in about 130 games a year; Berra in about 145. Second, the value of a run depends on how many runs it takes to win a game. Dickey played in an era when runs were plentiful and it took a lot of runs to win; Berra in an era when runs were not as plentiful and

Bill Dickey "learned" Yogi all of his experience, as Yogi would say in one of his earliest Yogi-isms — and Yogi surpassed Dickey as the greatest catcher in Yankees history, perhaps even in baseball history.

each one had more of an impact on a game.

Berra's Yankees never scored more than 914 runs in a season; Dickey's Yankees in various seasons scored 1,067, 1,065, 1,062, 1,002, 979, 967, 966 and 927. Dickey had one season, in 1939, in which he scored 10 percent of the Yankees' runs. Berra had seven seasons in which he scored 10 percent of the Yankees' runs, and two seasons, in 1950 and 1952, when he scored 13 percent of the runs. Dickey had four seasons in which he drove in 10 percent of the Yankees' runs, and one season, in 1937, when he drove in more than one-eighth of the total. Berra had 12 consecutive seasons, from 1948 to 1959, in which he drove in at least 10 percent of the Yankees' runs, and five seasons in which he drove in one-eighth of the total.

The test of greatness isn't just scoring a lot of runs. It's scoring a lot of runs and winning a lot of games and championships. Dickey played for teams that won seven of eight World Series; Yogi for teams that won 10 of 14.

Berra won the American League MVP Award three times, was in the top three in the voting six times, in the top five seven times, and was mentioned in the voting in 15 seasons. Dickey never won the award, was in the top three once, in the top five three times and was mentioned nine times.

Dickey was a great player. But Berra was better. Yogi was the greatest catcher who ever lived. That can be said with conviction because he was the only one who played every day, batted cleanup, did the job defensively and never had a bad season. Mike Piazza is a better hitter than Yogi was and never has a bad year, but Piazza's defense is lacking. Dickey was about as good as Berra, but he didn't play every day and he didn't bat cleanup. Roy Campanella was as good as Berra was in his best seasons, maybe better, and so was Bench and maybe Mickey Cochrane, too. Put all three together, and they had about as many great seasons combined as Yogi did by himself.

Josh Gibson was probably a better hitter than Yogi was and about as good a catcher, but it is unnerving to make judgements by relying on poorly documented records against a mix of uneven competition, which is the case with Gibson.

Yogi was a complete player: consistent and productive. If you are choosing a catcher on looks, take Carlton Fisk; on style, your man is Bench. If you want to win the pennant, choose Yogi.

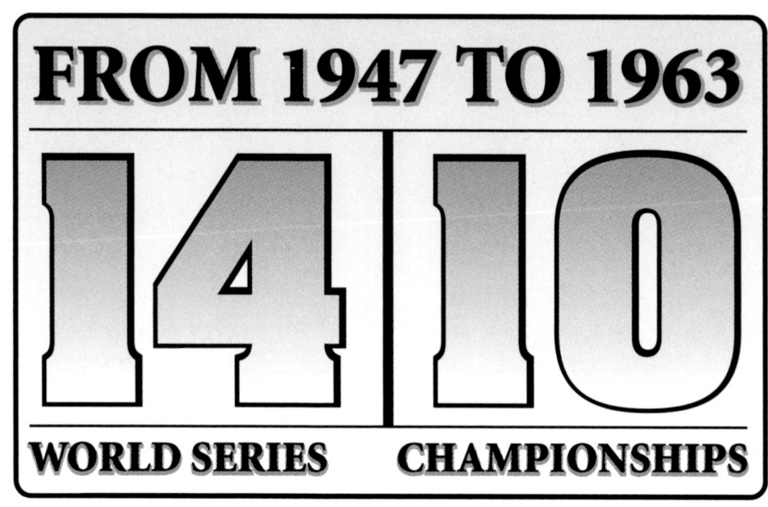

ELSTON HOWARD

It was a long march for Elston Howard. Almost 80 percent of major league players enjoy their peak three-year period by the age of 32. Howard was 32 before he really got a chance to catch.

Howard had to establish and prove himself in the Negro Leagues. The Yankees signed him, but then he had to spend two years in the Army. Upon his return, Howard had to prove himself in the minor leagues and play his way to the Yankees. By that time he was 26, and three obstacles still loomed large in front of him: He was the first African-American to sign with the Yankees Yogi Berra and Yankee Stadium.

Berra had run off Sherm Lollar, Gus Triandos and other competent catchers, and he was a long way from finished when Howard came along — Berra was just four years older than Howard. Yankee Stadium's spacious dimensions in left field and left center made it difficult for a right-handed batter like Howard to be successful. Howard didn't run well. He needed to hit home runs to contribute, and they required a prodigious poke if hit to the left side of the outfield.

Howard in 1962 had 18 home runs and 60 RBI in road games, and three homers and 31 RBI at Yankee Stadium. For his career, he hit more than two-thirds of his home runs on the road and drove in almost 100 more runs on the road than he did at home. In their road games, Howard had 69 percent more home runs than Bill Dickey did — in 350 fewer at-bats.

Like DiMaggio's numbers, Howard's statistics were adversely affected by his home park, and few have battled tougher competition for work. By 1959, however, Howard had earned enough playing time and was using it well enough to make the American League All-Star team. As Berra conceded that he could no longer catch 145 games a year, Howard more than picked up the slack.

It was noted earlier that Howard did not run well. He was one of those slow-moving but quick-reacting athletes, in the manner of Brooks Robinson. Howard had quick reflexes behind the plate and a great arm. He also had a way with pitchers; he understood them, and, more important, they understood him. By the time he got to play, he was a cagey veteran, more than prepared to thrive. From 1961 through 1964, Howard was the best catcher in the major leagues, a .300 hitter with power, and a defensive standout.

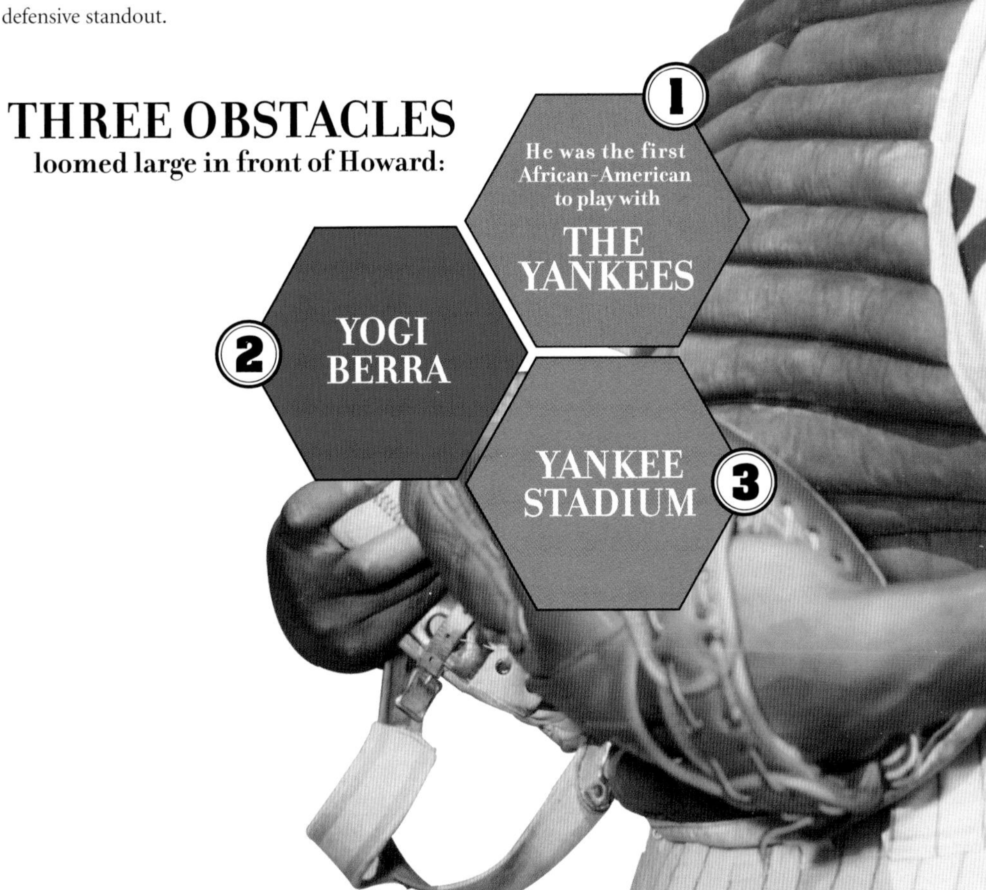

Like DiMaggio's numbers, Howard's statistics were adversely affected by his home park, and few have battled tougher competition for work.

BILL DICKEY

Bill Dickey was among the first modern catchers who hit well. He came to the major leagues at the end of an era when catchers almost always batted eighth. The practice of batting the pitcher ninth and the catcher eighth was adopted in the 1890s. There were very few catchers from 1895 to 1925 who did not bat eighth, even if they were good hitters, and there were extremely few catchers who were good hitters.

11
SEASONS WITH A .300+ BATTING AVERAGE

When the live-ball era—that's what it's called, but it's a misnomer — arrived in 1920, bunt attempts (which catchers were expected to chase) and stolen-base attempts dropped sharply. That reduced the defensive responsibilities of the catcher, and soon teams were focused on getting catchers who could contribute with the bat.

By the mid-1920s, catchers like Mickey Cochrane, Gabby Hartnett and Wally Schang had worked their way into the middle of the batting order, and then Dickey arrived to further the movement. Dickey was not Mike Piazza with the bat, and he was not Ivan Rodriguez behind the plate. He was not lightning-quick on defense, and he did not have the best throwing arm in the American League. He was a good left-handed hitter and could do the job defensively, and he improved steadily as he went along.

That really is what made Dickey special: He got better. For much of the 1930s, Yankees manager Joe McCarthy more or less used Dickey in a platoon. Open platooning was in poor standing with the players at that time. It would have been considered unmanly for, say, a left-handed hitter to acknowledge that he was better off on the bench against a left-handed pitcher. So managers rarely said they were platooning, but they did it all the same, usually in a sneaky fashion. On a day that a left-hander was to pitch against the Yankees, McCarthy would announce that Dickey was nursing a strained wrist, or whatever.

In 1936, Dickey learned how to pull the ball down the right field line and take advantage of Yankee Stadium's short fence. He had never been much of a power threat previously, hitting five to 15 home runs a season in his first seven years

with the Yankees, and with a fairly even split between home and road performance. But in 1936, he hit 22 home runs, 14 at Yankee Stadium, and the following two seasons his home-road splits were among the most disparate in baseball history, at least before there was a team in Colorado.

In 1937, Dickey hit .348 with 21 homers and 85 RBI at Yankee Stadium, and .315 with 8 and 48 on the road. In 1938, he hit .357 with 23 homers and 83 RBI at Yankee Stadium, and .274 with 4 and 32 on the road. For the two seasons, Dickey played in 136 games and batted 483 times at Yankee Stadium, and produced a .352 average with 44 homers and 168 RBI. His RBI rate for the 136 games was considerably better than Hack Wilson's in 1930 when he had 190 RBI, the major league record. Dickey hit two-thirds of his home runs in Yankee Stadium (135 of 202), although his batting average was seven points higher on the road than it was in New York.

The four-year stretch from 1936 to 1939 was one of the Yankees' greatest eras, and Dickey was right in the thick of the success. For those four years of jerking the ball down the right field line, he was a formidable player — and certainly an excellent player in the other years of his career. Dickey typified the Yankees in the wake of Babe Ruth; a team of men that took great pride in their professionalism, considered themselves the best in the business and went about beating the opposition in cold, workman-like fashion.

A close comparison of
Koufax and Ford

FORD		KOUFAX
16	Years Pitched	12
16/16	ERA better than league	7/12
15/16	ERA at least a half-run better than league	7/12
8/16	ERA a run better than league	6/12
5/16	ERA a run and a half better than league	3/12

WHITEY FORD

Quick now: Who had a better winning percentage: Whitey Ford or Sandy Koufax? Who had a better ERA: Ford or Koufax? Who had a longer career: Ford or Koufax? Here's a hint: This book is not about the Dodgers.

Ford had a better ERA (2.75 to 2.76), a better winning percentage (.690 to .655) and a longer career (438 starts to 314) than Koufax.

Koufax had immense impact on pennant races from 1963 through 1966 because he won 25 games and pitched 320 innings a year. If Ford had pitched 320 innings a year, how many games would he have won? Koufax, in his three Cy Young seasons, won one game for every 12.44 innings on the mound — a tremendous rate. Ford met or exceeded that standard in 1950, 1953, 1956, 1957, 1961 and 1963.

If you project Ford's win-loss records over 300 innings a year, these are his records for the first 14 years of his career: 24-3, 26-9, 23-11, 21-8, 25-8, 26-12, 19-10, 24-15, 19-14, 27-4, 20-9, 27-8, 21-7, and 20-16. Granted, Ford did not pitch 300 innings a season. My point is to illustrate the consistency of excellence with which he did pitch. Ford pitched in the majors for 16 seasons and had an ERA better than the league norm in all 16. Almost every year, he was half a run better than the league norm.

Ford gave up 1,107 runs in his career. A league-average pitcher facing the same number of batters that Ford faced would have allowed 1,528 runs — thus Ford was 421 runs better than average. Koufax was 282 runs better than average.

Ford's record was 236-106, 130 games over .500. No doubt, playing for tremendous teams influenced this phenomenal win-loss log. What would his record have been had he played for average teams? As best as can be estimated, about 214-128, a .626 winning percentage, which would rank among the top 50 since 1900.

Was any other pitcher in history as consistent at such a high level of performance as Ford? Warren Spahn, perhaps? Spahn had five seasons in which he won two-thirds or more of his decisions; Ford had 11. Spahn twice had an ERA a run better than his league's; Ford, eight times. Spahn's winning percentage, ERA and ERA compared to the league's are impressive, but they really are not in Ford's class.

Yankees manager Casey Stengel used a five-man rotation in an era in which almost every other team used a four-man rotation. He had plenty of pitchers to work with, and you can't argue with his results — but the system kept Ford from being a regular 20-game winner. Koufax retired at age 30; Ford pitched until he was nearly 40. You can't deny that advantage, either — but then, there were pitchers who worked 280 to 300 innings a year, and they didn't flame out after a few good years. We'll never know whether Ford would have been one of those.

Ford always was a star but never was considered a superstar, except perhaps in 1961. Benefiting from the new Yankees manager Ralph Houk using a four-man rotation that year, Ford went 25-4 and pitched 14 shutout innings in the World Series. Ford was as consistently good as anyone who ever pitched, but unfortunately history tends to favor the spectacular over the consistent.

ALLIE REYNOLDS

In 1947, his first season with the Yankees, Reynolds won 19 games and earned another victory in the World Series. He was with the Yankees for eight seasons, and he gave them eight outstanding seasons. His worst win-loss record with the Yankees was 16-12; other than that, he won at least 65 percent of his decisions every year.

Reynolds has almost the same career winning percentage and ERA as two other Yankees stars, Ron Guidry and Lefty Gomez, and all three pitched about the same number of innings. Reynolds' winning percentage is slightly lower than the other two's largely because he pitched four seasons for the Indians, during World War II. With the Yankees, his winning percentage (.686) is quite a bit better than Gomez' or Guidry's.

Reynolds' year-by-year record looks different than Guidry's or Gomez' for two closely related reasons:

❶

REYNOLDS MADE FEWER STARTS
and more relief appearances than Guidry or Gomez.

❷

Reynolds was a
20-GAME WINNER
only once.

In his autobiography, Casey Stengel listed Reynolds as the fourth-greatest player he managed, behind Joe DiMaggio, Yogi Berra, and Mickey Mantle (in that order), and ahead of Whitey Ford. Stengel wrote, "Reynolds was my greatest pitcher to start and relieve. He could warm up quick and was amazing in relief, amazing starting." As a reliever with the Yankees, Reynolds made 86 appearances and had a 15-9 record, 41 saves, a 2.87 ERA and averaged more than two innings per appearance. In 209 starts for the Yankees, he went 116-51 with a 3.35 ERA. Reynolds won 56 percent of his starts for the Yankees. Let's put that in context:

PLAYER	GAMES STARTED	WINS AS A STARTER	WINS PCT.
Walter Johnson	666	371	.557
Allie Reynolds*	209	116	.555
Warren Spahn	665	358	.538
Whitey Ford	438	227	.518
Sandy Koufax	314	159	.506

With Yankees*

Reynolds' numbers are even better if you include the World Series. He was 5-2 in nine starts, 2-0 and four saves in six relief appearances, with a sub-3.00 ERA in each role. Stengel couldn't decide whether he liked Reynolds better as a starter or a reliever, so he used him in both roles. That pattern of work compromised Reynolds' record. He didn't get enough starts to be a frequent 20-game winner, or make enough relief appearances to be remembered in the same vein as Goose Gossage.

Gomez had a better record than Reynolds as a starter, but as a reliever Gomez was 5-12 with a 4.24 ERA. Red Ruffing as a reliever was 9-15 with a 3.65 ERA, and Warren Spahn was 5-18 with a 3.68 ERA. The point is, switching back and forth between starting and relieving is a difficult role, and perhaps no one has done it as well as Reynolds.

RED RUFFING

Red Ruffing's career got off to a rather inauspicious start. He joined the Boston Red Sox in 1924 and by the time he was traded to the Yankees in May 1930, he had a 39-96 record—a .287 winning percentage. He is probably the only pitcher in history to have a record that poor and still have a job in the major leagues. Ruffing had just turned 26 when he joined the Yankees, and baseball fans remained excited about his potential for several reasons:

1 HE WAS A BIG MAN FOR THE ERA, STANDING 6-FOOT-1 AND WEIGHING MORE THAN 200 POUNDS.

2 HE COULD THROW **EXCEPTIONALLY HARD.**

3 **HE WAS A TERRIFIC ATHLETE.** IN ADDITION TO HIS PITCHING SKILLS, HE RAN WELL, WAS A FINE HITTER AND AN EXCELLENT FIELDER.

4 HE WASN'T AFRAID TO PUT THE BALL OVER THE PLATE **AND LET BATTERS HACK AT IT.**

The 1927 Yankees were one of the great teams in history, but that club's rotation unraveled in the subsequent few years. Herb Pennock, 19-8 in 1927, was 35 years old by 1929 and went 9-11 that year. Waite Hoyt, 22-7 in 1927, came up with a sore arm. Urban Shocker, 18-6 in 1927, died a year later. The Yankees, despite an offense that was stronger than ever, were dropping behind the Philadelphia A's and began scrambling for help. The Red Sox needed money, and Ruffing was available.

Ruffing's record with the Yankees over 15 years was 231-124 — a .651 winning percentage. The odd thing about his career is that when he was with a bad team such as the Red Sox, his record was far worse than his team's record; and when he was with a good team such as the Yankees, his record was better than his team's. Or maybe it is not odd at all. In his early years with the Red Sox, Ruffing really should have been in the minor leagues perfecting his craft. By the time he got to the Yankees, he had picked up a thing or two about pitching, including learning how to throw a sharp-breaking curveball.

In the early 1930s, Ruffing began experimenting with the pitch that now is called "the slider." It had various names at that time: sailer, tailing fastball, nickel curve. Whatever it was called, it was a good pitch if thrown properly, and Ruffing threw it probably better than anyone else of his time, in part because he was one of the few who threw it.

By the late 1930s, Ruffing was a perennial 20-game winner. As a bonus, he was one of the league's most reliable pinch-hitters, batting .364 in 1930, .330 in 1931, .306 in 1932, .339 in 1935, .307 in 1939 and .303 in 1941. He hit 36 home runs and 98 doubles in his career.

Ruffing was drafted into the military for World War II, although he was 39 at the time, and missed two years of baseball. By war's end he was ancient, yet he still could pitch. A sore arm prevented Ruffing from working regularly, but when he was able to take the mound he was highly effective. In 19 starts over 1945 and 1946, he went 12-4 with a 2.43 ERA. He no longer threw hard, but had become a wizened veteran who knew how to get by on guile and pain tablets. Twenty years after his career ended, Ruffing was elected to the Hall of Fame.

Ruffing's record with the Yankees over 15 years was 231-124 — a .651 winning percentage.

RON GUIDRY

Ron Guidry pitched a little bit for the Yankees in 1975 but spent most of the final two months of the season in the shadows of the bullpen, as the Yankees commenced the Billy Martin era.

Three years later, Guidry fashioned a 25-3 record with a 1.74 ERA and 248 strikeouts.

HOW GOOD WAS GUIDRY'S 1978 SEASON? NOTE THE FOLLOWING:

SINCE 1940, ONLY TWO PITCHERS HAVE FINISHED A SEASON 22 GAMES BETTER THAN .500: GUIDRY AND DENNY McLAIN, WHO WENT 31-6 IN 1968.

GUIDRY'S .893 WINNING PERCENTAGE IS THE ALL-TIME RECORD FOR A 20-GAME WINNER.

GUIDRY'S 1.74 ERA WAS EQUALED BY PEDRO MARTINEZ IN 2000. THEY ARE THE LOWEST ERAs IN THE AMERICAN LEAGUE SINCE THE END OF THE 1960s.

At the winter baseball meetings that December, the Yankees talked with the Pirates about a trade — the discussion led to the Yankees' acquisition of Willie Randolph — and the Pirates asked about Guidry being included in the deal. A few hours later, the Yankees talked with the Angels about a trade, and the Angels brought up Guidry's name. "I don't know who this Ron Guidry is," Billy Martin told the Yankees party as the Angels group left the room, "but we ain't tradin' him to anybody."

Guidry was a small, slender man, but very much a power pitcher, combining a mid-90-mph fastball with as good a slider as anyone has ever thrown. Guidry was late starting his major league career — he turned 27 in his first full season — and within a few years after his monster season he was making the transition to being more of a finesse pitcher.

Guidry's career has much in common with Lefty Gomez'. Both were reed-thin left-handers who had a big season early in their careers — Gomez was 26-5 with a 2.33 ERA in 1934. Both lost something off their fastballs in mid-career, survived a couple of seasons on instinct and guile, then re-emerged as 20-game winners without an overpowering fastball. Guidry spent his entire career with the Yankees; Gomez was with the Yankees for all but one game. Gomez started 320 games and relieved in 48; Guidry started 323 and relieved in 45. They have almost identical career winning percentages and ERAs (Guidry .651, 3.29; Gomez .649, 3.34). Gomez won 20 games four times, 18 once; Guidry won 20 games three times, 18 once. Guidry had seven straight seasons with a winning percentage better than .600; Gomez did that eight times in nine years. Each led the league twice in ERA, wins, and winning percentage. Gomez pitched 28 shutouts; Guidry, 26.

Gomez is in the Hall of Fame; Guidry isn't and probably won't be. Some argue that if Gomez is in, Guidry should be in, too. Both were exceptional pitchers, but neither is on a plateau with the greatest left-handers. Neither reached the brilliance of Sandy Koufax or Randy Johnson except in one season, and neither lasted long enough to afford his career the stature of Whitey Ford, Steve Carlton or Warren Spahn. Gomez was elected to the Hall of Fame in an era of profligate selections. He is far from being the worst pitcher selected — and Guidry was every bit as good as Gomez.

GOOSE GOSSAGE

In the midst of a run of spectacular seasons as a relief ace, Goose Gossage spent one miserable year as a starting pitcher. That was 1976 with the Chicago White Sox, whose manager was 68-year-old Paul Richards. If you think about it from Richards' perspective, you can understand where he was coming from. He was a major league catcher in the 1930s and 1940s, when pitchers with 90-mph fastballs were in the rotation, and old guys with dinky curveballs and herky-jerky deliveries were in the bullpen. To a man of Richards' generation, it was an article of faith that the best pitchers belonged in the rotation.

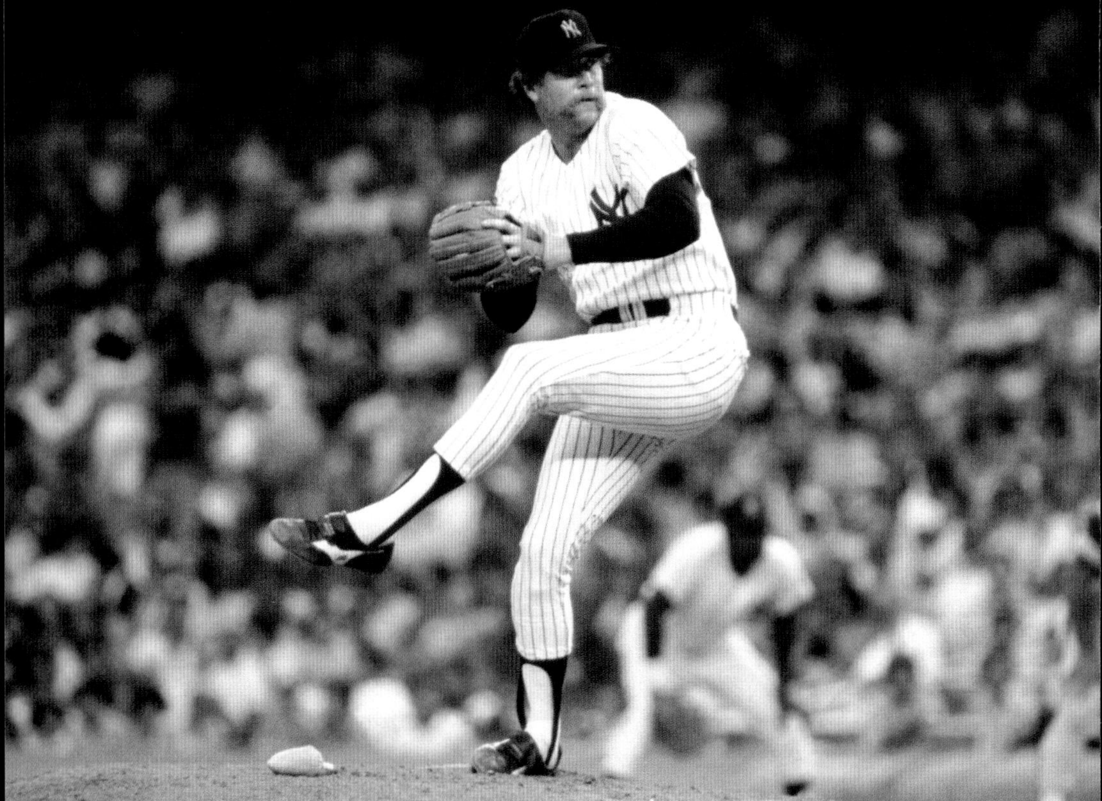

Relief pitchers and bullpen strategy have undergone numerous metamorphoses over the years. The way relievers are used now is quite different from the way they were used 10 years ago; and the way they were used 10 years ago was very different from the way they were used 10 years earlier. The bullpen has been an experimental lab since the 1920s, and each generation of managers has mixed the potion differently.

Gossage and the other great closers of his era — Dan Quisenberry, Sparky Lyle, Mike Marshall, John Hiller, Rollie Fingers — were the most valuable relief pitchers of all time. First, they pitched a lot more innings than modern relief aces. Gossage pitched 142 innings for the White Sox in 1975, 133 for Pittsburgh in 1977 and 134 for the Yankees in 1978. Lyle pitched 137 innings for the Yankees in 1977. Dennis Eckersley had an incredible 1990 season, but he pitched only 73 innings in 63 appearances. The top closers now pitch even less than Eckersley did. Second, the closers of the Gossage era worked more in high-impact situations than today's closers do. The modern closer usually works only in the ninth inning of a save situation. Often a save situation is not a high-impact situation — a team with a two- or three-run lead, with an inning to play almost always wins. The highest-impact situation is when the score is tied. Gossage and relief aces of his era often were summoned to work in tie games. That's why save totals then were not as high as they are now — Gossage led the American League in saves with totals of 27 (1978) and 33 (1980) — and why closers then had more decisions — Gossage was 10-11 in 1978 and 13-5 in 1983. In his six years with the Yankees, 1978 to 1983, he had 150 saves and a 41-28 record.

Gossage almost always pitched in the late innings when a game was close or tied. Comparing Gossage and Mariano Rivera "widely considered the top reliever in baseball history", Gossage pitched a larger number of innings and more critical innings. Thus, his impact had to be higher.

Gossage missed a good portion of the 1979 season because of a broken thumb, and by 1980 the concept of limiting the closer to save situations was sweeping baseball. Thus, Gossage never again worked 100 innings in a season, but he remained an effective pitcher into the early 1990s. He is one of seven pitchers that worked in 1,000 games — and perhaps the best in that group.

How long a pitcher lasts depends mostly on two things: his fastball and his health. Gossage had a great fastball and good health. He was a colorful, original, intimidating star, as memorable and effective a figure as has ever worked from the middle of the diamond in the late innings.

"When I cross the white lines, something clicks in me. I feel like no one can hit me. It's unbelievable how confident I feel. I turn mean. If my wife came out and looked in my eyes, she would say,

'WHO IS THIS GUY?'"

— GOOSE GOSSAGE

LEFTY GOMEZ

Yankee Stadium, built in the early 1920s, was designed to favor left-handed hitters for a reason so obvious that it doesn't need to be mentioned — OK, for Babe Ruth. However, it didn't immediately dawn on the Yankees that the park would also favor left-handed pitchers. The 1923 Yankees, the first to play in the Stadium, had only one left-hander — Herb Pennock — and their record in road games was six games better than their home record.

Gomez (far right) with 1937 World Championship teammates (from left) Frank Crosetti, Red Rolfe, Joe DiMaggio, Lou Gehrig, Bill Dickey, George Selkirk, Myril Hoag and Tony Lazzeri.

By 1929, the Yankees had numerous left-handed pitchers, but none of great quality. That same year, 20-year-old lefthander Lefty Gomez led the Pacific Coast League in ERA and won 18 games for the San Francisco Seals. The PCL of that era was stronger than any minor league since, boasting many players who were just as good as many in the major leagues. A 20-year-old leading the PCL in ERA would get your attention. The Yankees took notice and arranged to purchase Gomez' contract for $35,000.

Gomez was a skinny, nervous kid who could just throw hard. Not much of a curveball, no forkball, no change-up; just "Here it is. Try to hit this." His fastball had great movement as well as velocity. Gomez initially failed with the Yankees, but after picking up a curveball and learning to change speeds, he returned in 1931 and won 21 games, then 24 the next year.

Gomez had his greatest season in 1934, going 26-5 with a 2.33 ERA. This was the same season that Dizzy Dean won 30 games in the National League. Sportswriters of the time liked to sell baseball players as "characters." Lefty — like Dizzy — was all for it. If writers wanted to make him a character, that was money in his pocket, he reasoned. He became "Goofy"

Gomez, baseball's most famous and most successful after-dinner speaker. He concocted funny stories about things that supposedly had happened to him, made teammates the foils of his tales, and gabbed away as a guest speaker for 50 years. Literally hundreds of Gomez's anecdotes are part of the literature of baseball.

Gomez was a great deal more complicated than the cartoon character he made himself to be. The fact that he was funny and articulate gave the media much to write about, and masked the fact that among the great stars of that era, Gomez was the most difficult to live with. He was high-strung and had a terrible temper, and like all truly great players he had a low tolerance for defeat.

Gomez endured arm trouble in 1935 and 1936, and his fastball was not quite as fast anymore. He developed an effective slow curve and returned to form in 1937, going 21-11 and leading the league in ERA (2.33). Then he won 18 games in 1938. With apologies to Pennock, Gomez was the Yankees' first great lefthander. Only Whitey Ford among Pinstriper pitchers has had a better career than Gomez.

JACK CHESBRO

On the final day of the 1904 season, Jack Chesbro threw a wild pitch that allowed a run to score and prevented New York's American League team — then called the Highlanders — from winning the pennant. It is absurd to blame a pitcher who won 41 games for his team's failure to win the pennant, but this was an era of scapegoat sports journalism, a time when poor Fred Snodgrass and Fred Merkle became infamous for blunders on the playing field. Sportswriters rooted openly for the local team and felt they had to fix blame on someone when their team didn't win. Chesbro fell into that pit in 1904.

For the subsequent 25 years, Chesbro was more widely known for the wild pitch than for his 41-13 record, a victory total that proved to be the best of the 20th Century. At the time, however, 41 victories didn't seem out of the ordinary.

In the 1880s, 26 major league pitchers won 40 or more games in a season. A couple more did it in the 1890s. In 1904, those records were a part of the contemporary memory, as close to fans of that generation as Don Mattingly and Dave Righetti are to us. Thus, when Chesbro won 41 games in 1904, it did not have a tremendous impact on fans. The New York Giants had a 35-game winner and a 33-game winner the same season, and Ed Walsh of the Chicago White Sox would win 40 four years later.

When people began to research baseball history, some of the early historians thought the 19th Century records were too messy to bother with, and so they didn't. They drew an arbitrary line across history, recognizing only what happened from 1900 forward. That line made Chesbro the recognized record holder for victories in a season. Unfortunately, he was dead before he could enjoy his record. It truly is the American League record, because the AL didn't begin operations until 1901.

A case can be made that Chesbro's 41-victory season was the best season by a pitcher of that era, which is significant because his contemporaries included Walter Johnson, Cy Young and Christy Mathewson. He was as good a pitcher as they were for a year or two — Chesbro led the National League in wins in 1902 with 28, and in winning percentage in 1901 and 1902 — although his career achievement was not on their level. Chesbro was a regular starter for the Yankees from 1903 through 1908, compiling a 123-94 record. His winning percentage (.567) was greater than the team's (.503).

Chesbro was the first great pitcher with a spitball to his repertoire. The pitch was so effective that virtually every pitcher had adopted it by 1920; some threw nothing but a spitball. The proliferation of the spitball shaped the course of baseball, reducing runs scored to historic lows and driving strategy toward one-run gambits.

It was a spitball that Chesbro threw on the final day of the 1904 season that got away from his catcher, enabling a runner to score. The pennant went to Boston that day, and Chesbro would be haunted for the rest of his life. In the bigger picture, he was one of the fine pitchers of his day and among the best in Yankees history.

MARIANO RIVERA

To put the argument for Mariano Rivera as an all-time great closer in its strongest form, let's begin with a question: How many relief pitchers in history have had eight consecutive quality seasons like Rivera had from 1996 through 2003?

Answer: None. Rollie Fingers had seven straight, beginning in 1972, although a couple might have been of lesser quality; Bruce Sutter had seven straight, beginning in 1976; Goose Gossage had six straight, beginning in 1980; Lee Smith had seven straight, beginning in 1982; and Dennis Eckersley had six straight, beginning in 1987.

Hoyt Wilhelm, although he had more good seasons than any other reliever in history, never had more than five in a row. There are other guys you can argue for: Trevor Hoffman and Dan Quisenberry, among others.

Rivera has two credentials that enable him to be considered among the brightest of stars:

1) He is among a handful of closers who has been consistently excellent for several seasons in a row.

2) His performance in postseason play is probably the most brilliant of any reliever in history.

In modern baseball, the closer tends to get credit for what the team accomplishes, regardless of whether he deserves it. We constantly hear that a team cannot win a pennant without a top-notch closer, even though it happens frequently. We also hear often that the key to success in postseason play is a strong bullpen, even though there is little evidence that this is true.

There is some connection between a strong bullpen and postseason success. From 1980 through 2001, the team with the best bullpen in the playoffs — based on performance during the season using objective criteria — has won the World Series on seven occasions. The 1984 Tigers, 1985 Royals, 1986 Mets, 1988 Dodgers, 1989 Athletics, 1990 Reds and 1996 Yankees each entered postseason play with the best bullpen and won the World Series. In that same span, six teams that had the best bullpen didn't make it to the World Series: 1980 Yankees, 1982 Braves, 1991 Blue Jays, 1992 Athletics, 1997 Orioles and 1999 Mets.

It is true, of course, that successful teams tend to have good bullpens — just as they tend to have good second basemen, good left fielders, good catchers, etc. The upshot of all this? Rivera is a terrific pitcher, and he certainly deserves a measure of the credit for the Yankees' run of good seasons — but no more than Derek Jeter, Bernie Williams and Jorge Posada deserve. The Yankees have won a lot since the mid-1990s, and there is plenty of credit to go around.

GRAIG NETTLES

Perhaps the most intriguing question about Graig Nettles is why he never got credit for his defensive brilliance. You had to see him play third base to believe it. He could catch a line drive two feet into foul territory. He could knock down a ball several feet behind third, pick it up, and throw out the runner. A team that depends on left-handed pitching depends on its third baseman — and Billy Martin's Yankees had one of the best.

"I expect every ball to be hit to me. When I do that, **I'M NEVER SURPRISED.**"

— GRAIG NETTLES

There are two reasons why Nettles wasn't fully recognized as a defensive master craftsman. First, the American League was ankle-deep in Gold Glove–caliber third basemen: Nettles, Aurelio Rodriguez, Buddy Bell, Brooks Robinson, Sal Bando, Don Money. All were better defensively than any AL third baseman since. If someone raved about Nettles' defense, someone else could make a compelling argument for any other guy on the list. Second, Brooks Robinson. Although Clete Boyer was probably just as good a defensive player as Robinson, Brooks had established himself as the definitive glove man at third base by 1961 and had cemented that reputation with his spectacular play in the 1970 World Series. Furthermore, Robinson had parlayed his defensive reputation into a position as the league's most beloved star, the one player at that time who was cheered loudly in every park. Many were reluctant to accept that Nettles was as good a third baseman as God ever made, because ... what about our beloved ol' Brooks Robinson?

The failure to accept Nettles' excellence as a hitter is not hard to understand. It has to do with the misperception of statistics. The public was weaned on batting averages. For many people, a .250 hitter can never be the equal of a .300 hitter. Well, yes he can. A home run is a lot different from a single, and the batting average gives no credit for a walk, even though walks lead frequently to runs scored. Nettles hit .248 for his career, and for each 100 hits he had 57 runs scored and 59 RBI. Rod Carew hit .328, and for each 100 hits he had 47 runs scored and 33 RBI. If Nettles got 150 hits and Carew got 200, who was more valuable? Do the math: Nettles was going to score 80 runs and drive in 88; Carew 93 and 66.

Occasionally someone suggests Nettles for the Hall of Fame, and a chorus of catcalls is sure to follow: What was his batting average? How many Gold Gloves did he win? Suffice it to say that Nettles might have been the best .248 hitter who ever lived.

PHIL RIZZUTO

Phil Rizzuto was probably quicker on the double play than any other shortstop in history. We think a lot about a second baseman's ability to turn the double play; less about a shortstop's. In fact, the shortstop is the pivot man on the double play 82 percent as often as is the second baseman. If the shortstop isn't the pivot man, he often is the player who has to feed the ball to the second baseman, which means that his quickness and the timing of his throws is just as critical.

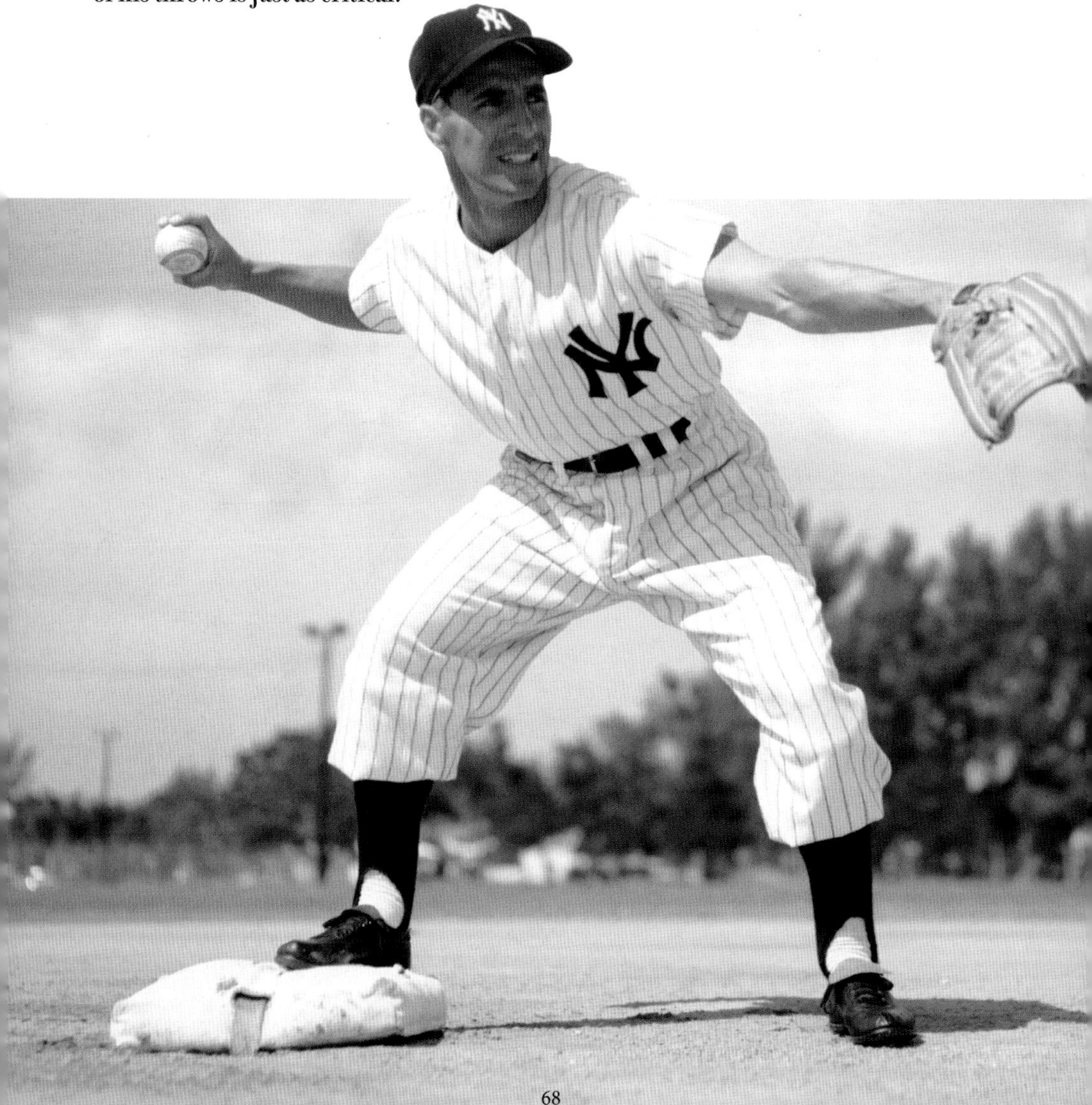

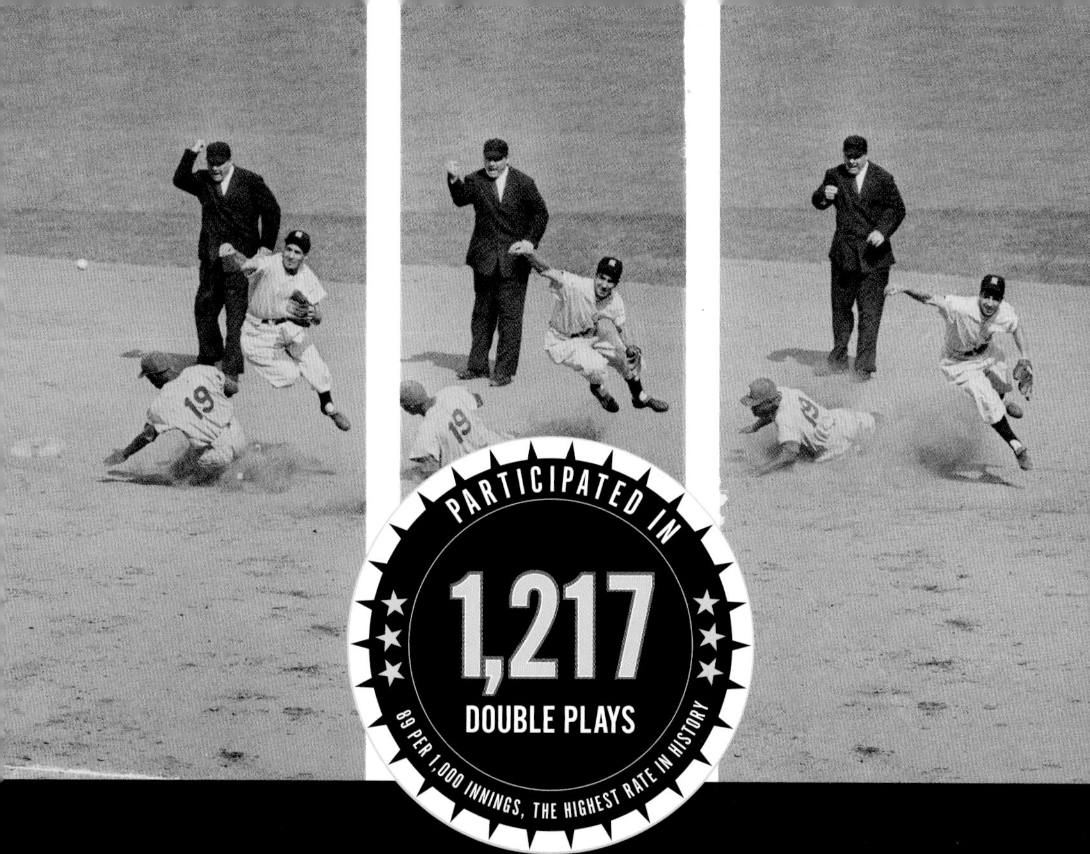

Turning the double play is a big part of a shortstop's role, and Rizzuto did that better than anyone else who ever played major league baseball. Playing shortstop in about 13,614 innings in his career, he participated in 1,217 double plays — 89 per 1,000 innings, the highest rate in history.

Baseball statistical analysts have complicated ways to estimate a team's "expected double plays" and thus determine whether an infielder turned a lot of double plays because he had many chances, or simply because he was good at turning the double play. Rizzuto was just good at turning the double play. Rizzuto and Joe Gordon probably were the best combination. But Rizzuto and Billy Martin were good, as were Rizzuto and Jerry Coleman, and Rizzuto and Gil McDougald.

Setting aside his double-play ability, Rizzuto still was a fine shortstop. He was quick and had a good arm when it was healthy, and his fielding percentages were extremely good. In his first two seasons in the major leagues, Rizzuto hit .307 and .284, averages that projected over a full career likely would have led to 2,500 hits. Rizzuto was in the Army for three years after that, and when he returned to the Yankees it took him five years to get his average back to .280. He hit .280 or better in only three seasons: the first two and his 1950 MVP year.

Rizzuto, who is in the Hall of Fame, had the subtle skills of a winning player. He was fast, a high percentage base-stealer, an accomplished bunter, and a terrific fielder. When he got on base, he kept moving. Rizzuto and Willie Randolph would have been an ideal double-play combination, except that they were almost too much alike.

Upon retiring, Rizzuto assumed an even more prominent role in the Yankees family, entering the homes of the team's fans as a broadcaster and becoming an emotional part of their attachment to the Yankees.

By most accounts, Rizzuto is low on the list of the great shortstops in baseball history. This, perhaps, should be the bottom line on him: He was the anchor of great, great teams.

DON MATTINGLY

When Don Mattingly joined the Yankees for the first time in 1982, there was little indication that he was going to be the first homegrown star in their everyday lineup since Thurman Munson.

By the standards of modern athletes, the 6-foot, 175-pound Mattingly was scrawny, and he did not run well. He had hit .300 everywhere he had played, but with single-digit home run totals and stolen-base numbers. The scouts, however, liked his defense.

Mattingly became the Yankees' regular first baseman in 1984, and he won the batting title that year with a .343 average. More surprisingly, he hit 23 home runs. That hardly is a significant number by today's standards, but in 1984 only eight American League players hit 30 home runs, and six batted less than the league average that year. Players who could hit .300 with power were more scarce than saints. Mattingly led the league in doubles, was near the league lead in extra-base hits, and drove in 110 runs.

In the following two years, Mattingly was often mentioned when discussion cropped up concerning who was the best player in the game. His 145 RBI in 1985 were by far the highest total in the major leagues in the 1980s. In 1986 he became the first major league player in 25 years to hit .350 with 30 home runs. He drove in 100 runs five times in the six seasons from 1984 through 1989, and led the major leagues in RBI during that period by more than 50. Mattingly had 684 RBI; second-place George Bell had 625.

As the 1990s dawned, Mattingly was essentially finished as one of the major league's biggest stars, done in by a chronic back problem. He played until 1995, but never again approached his achievement of the 1980s.

New Yorkers revered Mattingly. A native of Indiana, he was not urbane, sophisticated, or hip, but Yankees fans grew to appreciate his values and work ethic, and put him on the pedestal reserved for the storied franchise's true greats.

Mattingly played in an era when the press almost made a sport of baiting the Yankees, yet he was able to walk through controversy like a ghost through fire. Controversy and madness never touched him. He was neither a backstabber nor a target of it. Rather, Mattingly maintained a sense of decorum that had seemingly been passed down from the other great first baseman in Yankees history, Lou Gehrig.

MATTINGLY HAD THE HIGHEST SINGLE-SEASON RBI TOTAL OF THE 1980s
1985
145
RBI

"In big games, the action slows down for him where it speeds up for others. I've told him, 'I'LL TRADE MY PAST FOR YOUR FUTURE.' "

— **REGGIE JACKSON, on Derek Jeter**

DEREK JETER

Guessing where Derek Jeter's career will wind up is kind of like guessing whether an arrow in flight will hit the target. Or to use the baseball version of that analogy: It's like guessing whether a high fly will clear the fence. We really don't know. But we can avoid the pitfalls of history by not focusing on the destination of Jeter's career, and instead asking objective questions about his career thus far. Such as:

HOW MANY SHORTSTOPS HAVE PLAYED THIS WELL OVER A FIVE-YEAR PERIOD? About 10. Two shortstops have played at a distinctly higher level for a five-year period: Honus Wagner and Arky Vaughn. Eight others have played that long at a comparable level: Luke Appling, Ernie Banks, Lou Boudreau, Joe Cronin, Hughie Jennings, Cal Ripken Jr., Alex Rodriguez and Robin Yount. Some shortstops in the Hall of Fame — Pee Wee Reese, Phil Rizzuto, Ozzie Smith, Luis Aparicio, Joe Sewell and Dave Bancroft — never played as well for a five-year period as Jeter played from 1998 through 2002.

HOW MANY SHORTSTOPS HAVE HAD CAREERS COMPARABLE TO JETER'S AT THE SAME AGE? Five to eight, depending on how far you stretch "comparable." The certain five are Vaughn, Ripken Jr., Rodriguez, Yount and George Davis. If you want to stretch "comparable" a bit, add Cronin, Vern Stephens and Jim Fregosi.

HOW SHOULD WE EVALUATE JETER'S DEFENSIVE GAME? Everyone has their own take on it. What may be said without fear of contradiction is: a) His defensive statistics are not good; b) Defensive statistics contain many puzzles, are highly unreliable on an intuitive level, and are not terribly reliable even if you study them morning to night and know more about them than you know about your wife; and c) Jeter's defensive reputation is better than his statistics.

FOUR WORLD CHAMPIONSHIP RINGS

4 FOR 5

IN FIRST FIVE SEASONS

"JETER IS A SIX-TOOL PLAYER. I've never eaten with him so I can't tell you if he has good table manners, but Iwould imagine he has those too."

—JOHNNY OATES, former major league player and manager

NEW YORK
KC 4:05
PHI
SEA 4:05
PIT

WILLIE RANDOLPH

An appropriate title for a biography of Willie Randolph would be: *A Winning Type of Player.*

Tony Lazzeri is the only Yankees second baseman in the Hall of Fame, but many regard Joe Gordon, whose career was almost a continuation of Lazzeri's, the best of the Yankees at that position. Others maintain that Randolph was the best second baseman the Yankees have had.

Baseball is a percentage game; Randolph was a percentage player. Lazzeri and Gordon were power guys: athletic, strong, and possessing great arms. They were great players. Randolph rarely hit the ball hard. He didn't have a showy arm; you didn't see him zing the ball to third base and nail someone a foot off the bag, something Lazzeri could do. Randolph was best at taking what the opposition gave him and not making mistakes.

Lazzeri and Randolph played about the same number of games for the Yankees and had about the same number of at-bats. Randolph never scored 100 runs in a season, never drove in more than 67. Lazzeri scored 100 runs twice, drove in 100 runs seven times, and never drove in fewer than 67, which was his count in 1934 when he missed a month. On what basis could one argue that Randolph was a better player than Lazzeri? Five points:

OFFENSIVE CONTEXT The American League norm in Lazzeri's time was 5.1 runs a game; 4.4 in Randolph's era. If Lazzeri put 100 runs on the scoreboard and Randolph 90, Randolph would be ahead, based on how many wins he could purchase with the runs he created.

PLAYING TIME Randolph didn't score 100 runs because he would miss 20 games a year due to injuries, but he scored 99 runs in 138 games in 1980, and 96 runs in 120 games in 1987. If you focus on runs scored per game rather than per season, Randolph is ahead of Lazzeri. Randolph scored 75 runs more with the Yankees than Lazzeri did in about the same number of games.

CONTROL OF THE STRIKE ZONE Lazzeri struck out as much as he walked, which in his time gave him one of the poorer strikeout/walk ratios. Randolph played in an era when there were fewer walks and more strikeouts, yet he walked twice as often as he struck out, which gave him nearly the best strikeout/walk ratio of his generation. The only contemporary who had a better ratio was Wade Boggs, and not by much.

BASERUNNING Randolph stole 100 bases more than Lazzeri did, and was caught stealing almost the same number of times. That adds about 20 runs to Randolph's value, which isn't a lot. But there is a certain amount of base-running value that isn't documented in statistics.

DEFENSE Make no doubt, Lazzeri was a better hitter than Randolph was. So was Gordon, for that matter. But as he was when at-bat, Randolph in the field was quicker than Lazzeri and a better percentage player, too. Lazzeri turned 797 double plays with the Yankees and made 246 errors; Randolph had 1,233 and 183. By the standards of his time, Lazzeri was a fine second baseman. Until about 1930, second basemen were hitters first, defensive players second. That was true of Lazzeri, who came along at the end of that era. If he had come to the major leagues 10 years later, he would have been a third baseman. Randolph played at a time when the double play was more common, and therefore the ability to turn the double play was more important. Randolph had a larger defensive assignment — and he handled it.

The 1970s Yankees jelled in 1976, the year they added Randolph, and they ceased to be a winning team for several seasons when they let him go. Look at these win-loss records for the Yankees:

Five years before acquiring Randolph: **413-388 .516**	Last five years with Randolph: **445-364 .550**
First five years with Randolph: **489-317 .607**	First five years without Randolph: **376-433 .464**

At both ends of Randolph's career, the Yankees were 14 games a year better with him than without him. Yes, there are a million other factors that go into that; one player doesn't make a team. I'm not arguing that this proves Randolph was a winner, but these facts are irrefutable: The Yankees got better when they had Randolph; they got worse when they lost him.

Roy White

Roy White was as valuable to the Yankees in1972 as some Most Valuable Players — 19, to be exact — were to their teams. White in 1972 was as valuable as the 1987 MVPs in both leagues, George Bell and Andre Dawson. White in 1972 was more valuable than the 1995 AL MVP winner, Mo Vaughn.

White in 1970 was as good as or better than 60 percent of the players who have won MVP awards, including the AL MVP that season, Boog Powell.

White never hit .300, never hit 25 home runs, never drove in 100 runs. How can a player who didn't accomplish any of that in a season be rated for his career ahead of players such as Heinie Manush, Joe Carter, George Foster, Greg Luzinski, Kirk Gibson and Don Baylor?

Statistics can be interpreted intuitively, or they can be interpreted by careful logic. The logical interpretation of baseball statistics depends on finding the answers to two questions: How many runs did the player create?; and in his era and home park, How many runs did it take to win a game?

White created a large number of runs because he did a lot of things well. Let's compare him with Manush, who is in the Hall of Fame. Manush hit more singles, doubles and triples than White, but White hit more homers, drew more walks, and stole more bases. Comparing White with Carter, Carter hit more doubles and homers, but White hit for a higher average, hit more triples, drew more walks, stole more bases and was a better defensive player.

When you add everything together, White didn't create as many runs as Manush or Carter, but he doesn't trail them by much, either. What made White a better player than those men, in addition to his defense, is that he created a lot of runs in an environment where runs were scarce: in a pitcher's park in a pitcher's era. When runs are scarce, each run has more impact on a team's win-loss record. The runs White created, relative to the context in which he played, had more impact in terms of winning games than the runs created by Manush or Carter.

The problem is, no one remembers White as being an MVP-type of player. For that matter, no one thought of him in that light when he was playing. In 1970, when White had a better season than the AL MVP, Powell, he finished 15th in the voting.

Memory contributes immensely to our impression of players. Without a memory of White, or Mickey Mantle, for that matter, no one would care what their statistics were.

The problem with relying on memory when evaluating players is that memory doesn't always stand up under extensive questioning. If you saw White play, no doubt you gained an impression of him. But how many times did you see him play? 100 times? 200 times? Do you know? Did you see him play 10 percent of his games, or five percent? What did he hit when you saw him play? How many runs did you see him score, after he had worked the pitcher for a walk? How many subtle, nearly invisible contributions to victory did he make — when you saw him and when you didn't? If you are comparing White with Manush, you have to answer the same questions about Manush — and the truth is, you don't know most of the answers.

In many respects, White was a comparable player to Jim Rice. If you put them in the same park in the same season, most people would be able to see that. The impression that Rice was a fearsome, mighty slugger, and White was a quiet complementary player is not based on logical interpretation of their records. It is based on a generalized impression of their relative greatness as hitters, which really is based on a casual interpretation of batting statistics. A careful, logical interpretation leads to the truth, even if you don't want to believe that a team with White in its lineup was better off than a team with Rice in its lineup.

TONY LAZZERI

Tony Lazzeri grew up in San Francisco during the years of World War I. The kids in his neighborhood played baseball in Golden Gate Park about 350 days a year, and the games became quite competitive. The neighborhood kids included Joe Cronin, Wally Berger, Ernie Lombardi, Lefty O'Doul, Mark Koenig and, later on, Frank Crosetti. All made it to the major leagues; Lazzeri, Cronin and Lombardi made it to the Hall of Fame. Lazzeri was the star of those neighborhood teams. He was a year or two older than most of the others, bigger, stronger, the best hitter and the best pitcher.

Pacific Coast League

ALL WERE RECORDS FOR A PROFESSIONAL BASEBALL SEASON AT THE TIME

Lazzeri entered pro-ball in 1922 and within three years was playing shortstop for Salt Lake City of the Pacific Coast League, the major leagues of the West, so to speak. He hit 60 home runs, drove in 222 runs and scored 202 runs in 1925 — all records for a professional baseball season at the time. Lazzeri had the benefit of a 200-game season and the high altitude of Salt Lake City, but a lot of people had played long seasons and in great hitter's parks, too, yet no one previously had had a year quite like Lazzeri's in 1925. He committed 85 errors, but that hardly deterred the Yankees, who were rebuilding their infield after a mid-1920s swoon.

Lazzeri joined the Yankees in 1926 and was their regular second baseman for 12 years. Though he hardly had the physique of a slugger at 5-feet-11-inches and 170 pounds, Lazzeri was a prominent member of the "Murderers' Row" lineup. He reached 100 RBI seven times and 18 home runs four times. Italian-Americans who followed baseball took quickly to Lazzeri; he was their first superstar.

"He spoke seldom," author Frank Graham wrote of Lazzeri, "and when he did, his voice had an angry quality, although he was seldom angry." In 1936, Joe DiMaggio went east to join the Lazzeri and Crosetti doing the driving. During the long trip, DiMaggio asked Lazzeri if he had any advice. "Keep your mouth shut and play baseball," Lazzeri responded. Another year, Lefty Gomez made the cross-country drive with Lazzeri. A reporter asked Gomez if Lazzeri had said anything on the trip. "Just outside of Albuquerque," Gomez said, "I asked him if he wanted to stop for a hamburger. He said 'No'"

These stories could give the impression that Lazzeri was a dour man, which was anything but the case. He was quiet and intense, but he also had a great sense of humor and a warm smile — and was a notorious practical joker. A preacher used to visit the Yankees' clubhouse once a year and hand out copies of the Bible. On one occasion, a Lazzeri crony invited the preacher out onto the field to play catch. When the preacher returned to the clubhouse, he reached into his satchel for Bibles — only to find that the satchel now was filled with risqué French novels. Lazzeri had made the switch.

Lazzeri didn't have much time left after he retired from baseball. An epileptic since childhood, he had a seizure on the stairs in his home in 1946, and suffered a broken neck that ended his

CENTER *of Attention*

Few players have ever followed a greater star than Mickey Mantle did when he took over center field for the Yankees. Mantle not only designed his own Hall of Fame career on the same grass that Joe DiMaggio roamed, but he did it all with a style that defined the era as much as the man.

Commerce Comet

MICKEY MANTLE'S ETERNAL YOUTH

Essay by Peter Golenbock

I live with Mickey Mantle every day of my life. A large painting of his 1955 Bowman baseball card hangs on my office wall. It is spring training, exactly where, I do not know. The Mick is in his mid-20s, eternally young, the way he always looked when I was a youngster. He stands facing the camera, his muscles bulging, swinging a bat as he stares unsmiling straight ahead. He wears the Yankees' gray uniform, their road apparel. If the photographer's intention was to make Mantle look like a Greek god, then surely he succeeded. I was nine years old in 1955. Eisenhower was president in an age of suburban tranquility, cars with big fins, and the rise of Elvis. We lived in southern Connecticut, which was prime Yankees country. I came to idolize Mantle by listening to Mel Allen on my transistor radio at night, under the covers. In the den sat a boxy Dumont console, one of the first color TV sets. It looked just like the border of the 1955 Mantle baseball card. On that TV, I first saw the broad back, the muscular arms, and the powerful swing. It was from watching Mantle that I decided on my life's goal: to succeed him as the center fielder of the New York Yankees.

The young Mantle with his father, Mutt.

Whenever I played hit-the-bat or home run derby, I switch-hit like Mantle did, and I ran the bases imitating Mickey's powerful lope. Against the Early Wynns of the neighborhood, I banged tennis balls out of my yard like I imagined Mantle would have. After hitting one far over the pine trees and through a neighbor's second-floor window to the accompaniment of the tinkle of broken glass, to win a one-o-cat game in the bottom of the ninth, I ran the bases with dignity, refusing to indulge in a flashy orgy of celebration, because Mickey never did.

When I woke up in the morning, I knew it was going to be a great day because the odds were heavy that the

> "I always wished my dad could be somebody else than a miner."
>
> – MICKEY MANTLE

"When he took BP everybody would kind of stop what they were doing and watch."

— JIM KAAT, former pitcher

Yankees were going to win and that Mickey was going to do something memorable, whether it was to hit a towering home run or make a running catch or throw a runner out at home or even lay down a bunt and beat it out with his surprising speed.

For my generation of Yankees fans, to call Mickey Mantle a hero would be to understate reality. Mantle wasn't just a star ballplayer. He was an integral part of our lives, like my Aunt Eva, who brought me silver dollars from Las Vegas every time she visited. Mickey was almost a religious figure, because for the length and breadth of my childhood he was one person who never let me down and often gave me more joy than any human being had a right to experience.

Off the top of my head I can remember a few of the Mick's most glorious moments:

- The home run he hit off Chuck Stobbs in Griffith Stadium in Washington, D.C., that soared out of the stadium and landed — according to legend — some 565 feet from home plate.
- The running catch he made of a Gil Hodges drive in the fifth game of the 1956 World Series that saved Don Larsen's perfect game.
- The ball he hit against Pedro Ramos of the Washington Senators in May 1956 that banged against the upper façade of Yankee Stadium, three feet short of becoming the first fair ball hit out of the Stadium.
- The home run he hit against Barney Schultz in the bottom of the ninth to beat the St. Louis Cardinals in the third game of the 1964 World Series.
- His two home runs and five RBI in Game 2 of the 1960 World Series against the Pittsburgh Pirates. He would hit 18 home runs in his 12 World Series, a record that I consider the most significant of all baseball records.

Not everyone in my neighborhood was a Yankees fan. Pauly Housman rooted for the Dodgers — the Brooklyn Dodgers — and he would argue that his center fielder, Duke Snider, was a better player than the Mick. "Duke has to play in Ebbets Field, which is death to left-handed hitters," Pauly would say, "and look at all the home runs Duke hits."

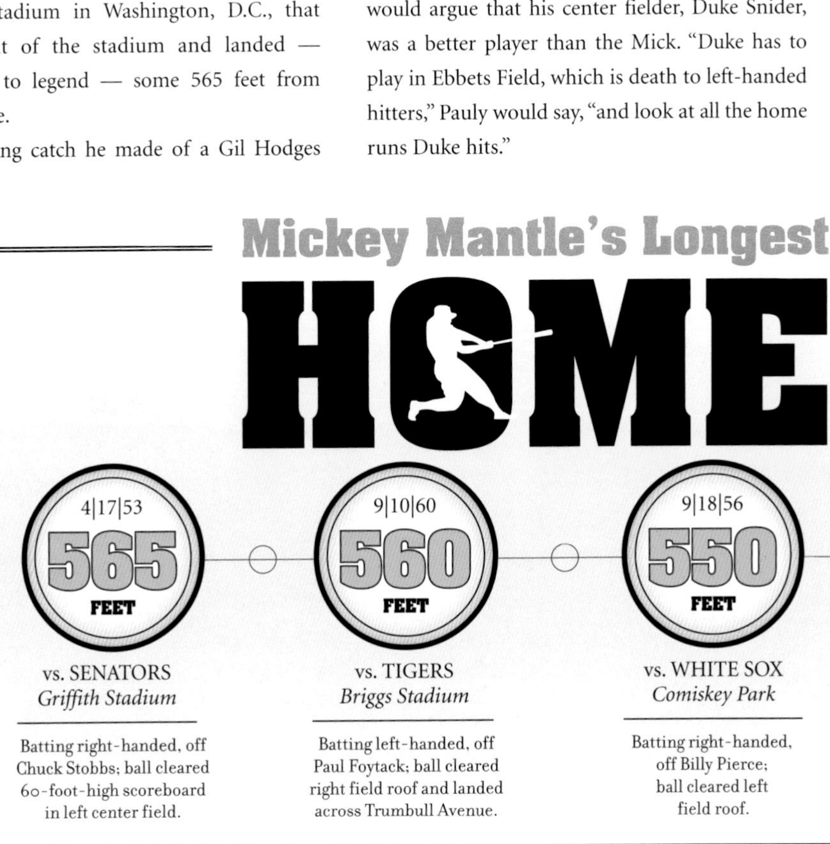

I would respond, "But Mickey plays in Yankee Stadium, where it is 467 feet to center field, and look how many home runs he hits."

Another friend, Bobby Nemiroff, would tout the skills of his favorite New York center fielder, Willie Mays of the Giants. "Mays can hit better than Mantle, and he can field better than Mantle, and he can throw better than Mantle," Bobby would say, and soon I would want to grab him by the throat and choke him until he stopped breathing.

But I never did because on some level I knew that if Snider and Mays were Peter Lorre and Edward G. Robinson, Mantle was Clark Gable, a superstar whose fame transcended the game. Dodgers fans loved Snider; Giants fans loved Willie. But around the country, fans from California to Maine, Florida to North Dakota, loved Mantle. One reason was that every fall when the nation tuned in to the World Series, the Yankees almost always were in it, and the star of the production almost inevitably was Mantle. If you lived in Oklahoma or Kentucky or any place that didn't have a major league team, there really was only one hero for you, and that was Mantle. Kids across America wanted to hit like him, tried to run like him, even delighted in striking out like him. As the medium of television grew, the legend of Mickey Mantle grew with it. Mantle's stature hardly wilted in retirement. Rather, it continued to grow and reached iconic proportions. No major league ballplayer since has held greater sway with the public. And with his death in 1995, he became a saint in some quarters. My office, practically a shrine to the Mick, is evidence of that.

As a kid, whenever I argued with Dodgers and Giants fans over the relative merits of our stars, I had verbal ammunition to shut up everyone. If noting that Mantle had won the American League's Most Valuable Player trophy three times wasn't enough, I would make my recitation in sort of a mocking sing-song, and by the time I was 18 it went like this: "1951, 1952, 1953, 1955, 1956, 1957, 1958, 1960, 1961, 1962, 1963, 1964."

Those were the years Mantle led the Yankees to the pennant. You think the Yankees have a lock on the American League today? Joe Torre's boys still have a long way to go to match the Mantle years.

3
AMERICAN LEAGUE
MVPs

1956
1957
1962

CAREER TOTALS

GAMES
2,401
AT BATS
8,102
RUNS
1,677
HITS
2,415
DOUBLES
344
TRIPLES
72
HOME RUNS
536
RUNS BATTED IN
1,509
WALKS
1,733
STRIKEOUTS
1,710
STOLEN BASES
153
BATTING AVERAGE
.298

"It was all I lived for, to play baseball."

– MICKEY MANTLE

But all dynasties come to an end, and for the final five years of his career Mantle played on bad teams. No one lasts forever, not even the Mick. His legs grew tired and his swing slowed, and on June 8, 1969, proclaimed by New York City mayor John V. Lindsay as "Mickey Mantle Day," Mantle came to Yankee Stadium to say goodbye. I went. So did 65,000 of my closest friends.

After being introduced by the Voice of the Yankees, Mel Allen, Mantle left the dugout and started onto the field, and everyone began clapping with great fervor. I couldn't help thinking that maybe if we clapped long and loud enough, he would come back and play again.

He received a nine-minute standing ovation, the longest ever heard at the Stadium. The fans were asked to stop. Mantle, wearing a conservative dark suit, stood in front of a bank of microphones and soaked up the love from his teammates and fans as his hallowed uniform No. 7 was retired.

He told the throng, "Playing 18 years before you folks is the greatest thing that ever happened to a ballplayer. It's been a great honor. I'll never forget it. Thank you very much." It was simple and heartfelt.

Pat Summerall, the master of ceremonies that day, said, "Happiness is Mickey."

Mantle then slowly rode around the perimeter of the field in a white golf cart and waved. An entire generation of Yankees fans — Mickey fans — waved back and became teary-eyed as we said our thanks for 18 years of thrills and excitement. We also were crying because his retirement marked the official end to a Yankees dynasty. And to our youth. Where had that nine-year-old boy gone? He had gone to law school. I never did succeed Mantle in center field, of course. Bobby Murcer did. At age 13 I discovered what most kids find out: Mere mortals cannot hit the curveball.

In the summer of 1972 I was hired by the Prentice-Hall publishing company in New York to be an editor in their legal publications department. After two months I was bored, and so I walked down to the company's trade book division and talked myself into a contract to write a book on my Yankees. If I had picked any other subject, I am convinced I would have been unceremoniously shown the door. I had never written a book. What made me think I could do it? My love of the Yankees, that's what.

I knocked on the door of the editor of the trade books division. He ushered me in. "I have an idea for a book," I said. It turned out he was almost as rabid a Yankees fan as I was. We shook hands on a contract. A career was born.

The Yankees at the time were owned by CBS and run by Michael Burke, a man who promoted the arts. Team officials were kind enough to let me hang out in the bowels of Yankee Stadium throughout the 1972 season and do my research, which included pouring through their vast archive of newspaper articles. During that time, I got a chance to meet Mantle a couple of times when he came to the Stadium for Old-Timers games and special appearances.

One time Mantle, several teammates and I were in the Stadium Club at about 11 in the morning before an Old-Timers game. What I noticed most about Mantle was that he was uncomfortable being treated as a celebrity. Fame was an enemy. He shied from the limelight and refused to allow others to treat him as someone who was special. Away from the demands of reporters and fans, Mantle appeared relaxed and charming, and at home with former teammates, who clearly loved him. Whenever he laughed, the entire room laughed with him.

After a year of reading newspaper articles, I decided I had no better idea of who these ballplayers were as men than when I began. The articles I had read about Mantle gave no hint of his charm, warmth, and love of laughter. I decided that to write my book, I would need to interview them, a decision that would change my life. It's 30 years later, and interviewing athletes continues to be one of the great pleasures of my life.

I traveled from coast to coast, seeking out the heroes of my childhood. Almost always, the talk would come around to Mantle. As I had observed, his teammates loved him dearly, despite his insecurities. Being his friend was important to them. When they talked about him, it was always with a twinkle in their eyes. It was clear that he had been their hero as well as mine.

I went to see Tom Sturdivant, who had pitched for the Yankees from 1955 through June 1959, when he was traded to Kansas City. When I interviewed him at his home in Oklahoma City, he made it clear how much he loved playing for the Yankees and being friends with Mantle.

"To me, Mickey Mantle was the Yankees," Sturdivant said. "You know the people came out to see the Yankees, but the people really came out to see Mantle. Mantle was the greatest ballplayer walking.

"I'll tell you a funny story. It was in Yankee Stadium after I had been traded to the Athletics. The night before the game Mickey and I go out for dinner, and he says, 'You know, Tom, you're the only right-handed pitcher who has enough control that I'd hit righty off of, and I believe off of you I could hit one completely out of Yankee Stadium.'

September 16, 1951, New York Yankees outfielder Mickey Mantle, the first man to face Bob Feller in the first inning. Mantle, the 19-year-old switch-hitting rookie, flied out on the play, but the Yankees outscored the Cleveland Indians 6-1, putting themselves back in first place in the American League.

"Actually, that got to me a little, putting it to me the way he was. So I said, 'I'll tell you what, Mickey. If the ballgame's not at stake, now I'm not going to take anything off of it, but if you walk up there right-handed, I'll reach back and let you have the best fastball I've got, letter-high, and right down the middle. We'll just find out whether you're a better hitter or I'm a better pitcher.' And he said, 'You're on.'

"Well, the next day we get way behind and sure enough, here comes ol' mop-up man Sturdivant in to pitch for the Athletics, and Mickey steps into the batter's box as a right-handed hitter. Our manager, Eddie Lopat, he whistles, which is the curveball sign. Lopat at that time had an automatic fine if he called a pitch from the bench and you didn't throw it. I was shaking my head trying to tell Lopat my shoulder hurt. He whistles again and sticks up some money in the air like he's going to fine me. So the first pitch I throw Mickey is a big ol' roundhouse curveball, and Mickey, he runs clear out of the batter's box. And he is some kind of mad sum'bitch.

"He gets up there again, and Lopat whistles again. Well, instead of throwing him a curveball, I throw him a slider, which is a halfway fastball. He hits a line drive, and our center fielder, Bobby Del Greco, runs out to the monuments and catches it.

"If I knew I would live this long, I would have taken better care of myself."

— MICKEY MANTLE

Remember, he has to hit the ball clear out of the ballpark to win the bet. But anyway, it's caught. And he runs to first and makes a circle and comes runnin' back at me.

"I had already given him the mound. I wasn't going to stand on that mound and let that freight train run over me. Aw, he was mad, and everybody was giggling on our bench because they knew what was going on.

"Later on, he said this was one of the funniest experiences of his career, me throwing him the big ol' curveball. Crossing him up, you know. Good ol' Tom. Ol' buddy Tom. Really, I didn't have enough curveball that he couldn't hit it anyway. In fact after that first one, what he said to me was, 'Throw that damned curve again, and I'll kill you with it.' And he tried to. Only thing, he hit it too high." And Sturdivant let out a hearty laugh.

Mantle's teammates recalled how he played in pain late in his career, as his injuries took a toll. But he never complained, they all said. He just went out every day and did his job to the best of his ability.

In doing the research for the book, I decided to travel to Commerce, Okla., where Mickey grew up. I wanted to see his hometown with my own eyes. The solitude of the barren town was eerie. The buildings were one story, and only the leafy green elm trees prevented you from seeing forever. A young boy in tattered blue jeans rode by on a too-small bicycle. He was carrying his fishing pole. No cars passed by the gasoline station.

Mantle's childhood home was only a stone's throw from the hulking gray power plant that once sent energy into the Blue Goose Mine where the Mantle family had worked. The mine was abandoned, but the awesome pyramids of waste materials stretched as far as the eye could see, giving the area a surreal quality. Deep cavernous quarries, filled with rainwater, were dug as far into the ground as the mounds were high. Only an occasional hearty tree was interspersed among the barrenness. The Mantle home was also abandoned. All the windows were broken. The white paint had peeled. The house was built, it seemed, for dwarves. You had to bend down to go into the kitchen. There was only one bedroom, where Mickey, his older brother, his half-brother, his younger twin brothers and his sister all slept. Mantle had been a poor kid.

When Mutt Mantle was not in the mines, he was usually making his son into a baseball player. The story has become legend. When Mickey came home from school, he went to work, playing baseball. His father and an uncle who threw left-handed took turns teaching him to switch-hit. The incessant practice paid dividends.

The closest major league teams to northeast Oklahoma, where Mantle grew up, were the Cardinals and the Browns in St. Louis. Cardinals scout Runt Marr decided the 5-foot-7-inch teenager was too small, and a tryout with the Browns was cancelled because of heavy rain. When Mantle graduated from Commerce High, the only scout willing to sign him was Tom Greenwade of the Yankees. Mantle got $1,000, and Greenwade became famous.

When Mantle first joined the Yankees in 1951, he was a child — timid, self-conscious and completely overwhelmed. He took one look at the Empire State Building and stood in open-mouthed awe. His world had been poling for catfish on the Neosho River, working in the lead-zinc mine, or walking through a grassy field with a piece of straw between his teeth. That he was able to succeed in New York speaks of his talent. That he was able to replace the legendary Joe DiMaggio in center field does, too. Despite his humble upbringing, Mantle was quickly able to capture the hearts of all of New York City. A generation of Yankees fans cannot only picture his face from the baseball cards, they can also tell you the statistics on the back of the cards. We can all recite the grandest line by heart: .353, 52 home runs, 130 RBI, 132 runs scored. Those were Mantle's major league–leading statistics in 1956, his greatest season. When he retired, he had 536 home runs, more than all but two other players in major league history.

I had plenty of background information for my book. Now it was time to interview Mantle at length. Bob Fishel, the Yankees' public relations director, made the arrangements for me. I opened the steel-gray door leading into the Yankees clubhouse, and I asked Pete Sheehy, the clubhouse attendant, where I could find Mantle, who was in New York for a commercial endorsement. Sheehy pointed to the far end of the room. Mantle, dressed in buckskin — he lived in Texas — stood by a wall mirror combing his blond hair. All that was left for me to do was introduce myself.

I couldn't do it. Mantle had been my hero in so many ways. I wore No. 7 on my Camp Winaukee uniform. When I went to the dentist and suffered through a brutal drilling, I would imagine that Mantle had hit a home run and was running around the bases. Usually by the time he crossed home plate, the drilling was over. How could I approach a man who had saved me so much pain?

I asked Elston Howard, who I had interviewed, to make the introduction. Howard was kind, and he told Mantle about the book I was writing. Mantle asked me about several of his former teammates, whether I had seen them, how they were doing. I asked him if we could chat. He put his arm around my shoulder and with a straight face said, "No."

I was stunned. Then his face broke into a wide grin, and he laughed. "Where do you want to do this?" he asked. We sat on a table at the far end of the Yankees clubhouse.

It was 1973, and Mantle had not yet become a media darling. He still had a reputation for surliness and occasional hostility toward the media. When he first came up, in 1951, he was self-conscious of his Oklahoma twang and his lack of education, and like DiMaggio before him, he was wary of the pushy, garrulous reporters. In an attempt to avoid controversy, he said little or nothing. It was the pre–*Ball Four* era, and reporters talked of his prodigious feats rather than about his boorish behavior. I was keenly aware that Mantle had little patience for interviews or photograph sessions when he was a player. "How much longer is this going to take?" he would bark.

But on this summery May afternoon, Mantle was in a bubbly, effusive mood. He was happy to be

"He [my father] had the foresight to realize that some day in baseball that left-handed hitters were going to hit against right-handed pitchers and right-handed hitters were going to hit against left-handed pitchers; and he taught me, he and his father, to switch-hit at a real young age, when I first started to learn how to play ball. And my dad always told me if I could hit both ways when I got ready to go to the

back in New York, at Yankee Stadium. I stood in awe as I began asking him about the fabric of his life.

I knew that his father had worked in the Blue Goose Mine in Commerce, and I began by asking him what his father's job entailed. Mantle talked softly and slowly with a drawl he never did lose. "He started out as a shoveler," Mantle said, explaining that the lead veins were blasted out at night and a crew came along the following day and shoveled the chunks into big cans. "I don't know how big a can is, but it's a very big can. And he was able to shovel, like, 50 cans a day, which was great," said Mantle, his voice welling in pride.

"Did you work with your dad in the mines?" I asked.

"Yeah. I worked in the mines the last two years of high school. In fact, when I joined the Yankees in 1951 I was still working in the mines. I was a screen ape. That's the guy that stands over the boulders that come by that go through a screen, and if they're too big you have to beat them up with a sledgehammer. Everybody thinks I lifted weights or something, because when I first came up I was built good."

I asked him about the knee injury he suffered in the 1951 World Series stepping on a drainage gate in the outfield. "They took me to the hospital, and that's when I found out Dad was sick," Mantle said. "My dad was sitting on the side of me in the cab to the hospital. My knee had swelled up so bad I couldn't move it. Dad got out of the cab first, and I put my arm around his shoulders to jump out of the cab, put my weight on him like this," — and Mickey leaned on me, his strength weighing heavily on my left shoulder — "and he just collapsed on the sidewalk. They call it Hodgkin's Disease. It had eaten up his whole back. My mother told me later that he hadn't slept in bed for a year. But he never would tell me about it. That's the first I ever knew he was sick." Mantle screwed up his face and sighed.

"I got operated on," he said, "and then we went home, and he went back to work, and I could tell he was really sick then. I was told to take him to the Mayo Clinic, so when I got well I took him up there, and they cut him open and sewed him back up, and they said, 'Just let him do whatever he wants to. He doesn't have much longer to live.' He went back to the mines. He worked until about a

major leagues, that I would have a better chance of playing. And believe it or not, the year that I came to the Yankees is when Casey started platooning everybody. So he did realize that that was going to happen someday, and it did. So I was lucky that they taught me how to switch-hit when I was young."

— **MICKEY MANTLE, excerpt from his Hall of Fame induction speech**

NY

month before he died, in the spring of 1952."

Mutt Mantle was 39 when he died, and his famous son thereafter carried a fear of early death. An uncle also had died young. Hank Bauer once arrived in the Yankees clubhouse and noticed that Mantle was rather hung over. Bauer suggested to Mantle that he should stay home more and take better care of himself. Mantle looked at Bauer through bloodshot eyes and said, "My father died young. I'm not going to be cheated."

Mantle was 36 when he retired, his body too broken to continue. For the rest of his life he was tormented by the realization that he never again would play the game his father had taught him. He was elected to the Hall of Fame in 1974 and welcomed the honor, but Mantle was never impressed by his accomplishments or any of the rewards, trophies and honors that came with them. He would have traded everything, including his three Most Valuable Player awards, to again be able to cavort with his teammates, to be able to hit long home runs, to hear the adulation of ballpark crowds. When Mantle drank, it was not to cheat death, but to cheat reality.

"I miss baseball," Mantle said softly. "Since I've been away from it, I keep having nightmares. I always dream that I'm trying to make a comeback, and I can't hit the ball, and it pisses me off." Mantle was wringing his hands as we spoke. "Pitchers throw me fastballs, and I just can't hit them anymore.

"There's another nightmare. I'll be outside Yankee Stadium trying to get in, and I can hear them announcing my name on the loudspeaker, for me to hit, and I'm outside and I can't get in. I hear Casey Stengel asking, 'Where's Mickey?' But I can't get in. Those are my two bad dreams."

He had another thought. "I always felt that I was really overpaid. Whitey [Ford] and I figured out that I had 1,700 walks and 1,800 strikeouts. That's a total of 3,500. And if you get up 500 times a year, you figure I spent seven years where I never hit the ball!" Mantle laughed raucously.

"People think that I was always hurt," he said with a sigh, "but I played for 18 years. I played more games as a Yankee than anyone else who ever played for them." An overwhelming sense of sadness seemed to engulf Mantle, who was just 41 at the time.

"You know," he said, "I miss playing very much."

That sense of sadness never left him. For the final 25 years of his life, he no longer could play baseball, and to ease the pain he medicated himself with drink. It was only after his son Billy died of alcoholism that Mantle decided to come clean. He not only came to grips with his alcoholism, but he had the grace and hero's dignity to go on TV and talk about the danger of drinking, telling young kids, "Don't be like me." His bravery made us love him even more.

In 1995 we found out that Mantle needed a liver transplant. He got a new liver that June but was dead two months later of cancer, leaving us children of the 1950s and 1960s with a feeling of deep sadness and a lifetime of memories.

When I need to smile, I think back to the summer of 1961, when Mantle and Roger Maris were capturing the hearts of baseball fans all over the country as they pursued the most hallowed of baseball records: Babe Ruth's 60 home runs from 1927. I recall sitting on the white sand at Bradley Beach, N.J., listening to my palm-sized Magnavox eight-transistor radio in a brown carrying case. The sun was bright, the water was refreshing, and the Yankees were playing a doubleheader. Mantle and Maris and John Blanchard made mincemeat of the opposition.

What Mantle and those Yankees teams meant to me is never far away, and I'm sure others just like me feel the same way. Mantle and Maris are an indelible part of my psyche. They are gone now, but my good friend Andy Jurinko painted for me a portrait of the Yankees outfield of my youth. And there on canvas, for all eternity, is the greatest outfield the Yankees ever had, at least in my mind — Mantle, Maris and yours truly, Peter Golenbock.

Mickey Mantle

Among the four great superstars of Yankees history, Mickey Mantle is the eternal adolescent. He came to the major leagues as a 19-year-old of seemingly limitless ability – and no matter what he accomplished, he would always be regarded by many as the player who was supposed to be better.

Mantle was almost 6 feet tall, blond, strikingly handsome, broad-shouldered, immensely powerful and able to accelerate instantly and run like the wind for a short distance. He was a likeable man with a ready wit and an easy-going manner. We also can say he was a "natural hitter," a result of countless hours of batting practice he took in his youth from either side of the plate, depending on whether his father or his uncle was pitching. Mantle could read a curveball when he was 19.

When Joe DiMaggio retired, Mantle stepped in as the Yankees center fielder, a mantel — pun intended — which should not be wished even upon one's enemies. Mantle became a greater player than DiMaggio. The differences between the two are fairly subtle. Mantle's .298 batting average is about as impressive, in the context of his time, as DiMaggio's .325, or, for that matter, as Babe Ruth's .342 and Lou Gehrig's .340. Mantle batted .298 in a time when the American League

—**AL KALINE**, responding to a taunting fan who said Kaline was not half as good as Man

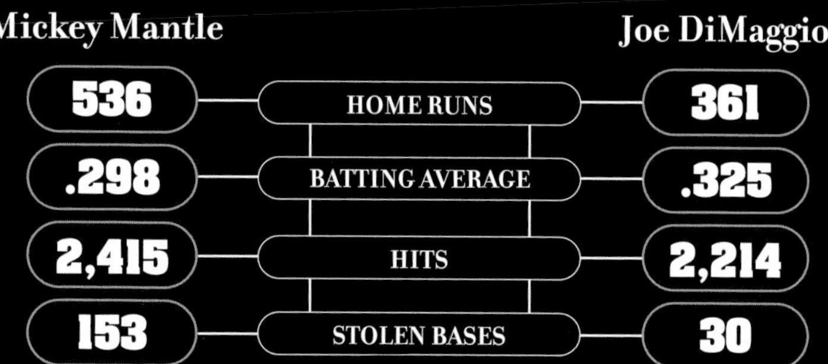

batting average was .256; DiMaggio hit .325 in an era when the league averag was .276. Adjusting both to a league average of .270, Mantle's average would b about .314, DiMaggio's about .318, Ruth's .324 and Gehrig's .322 — not reall much difference.

Nor is there much to separate Mantle and DiMaggio in terms of power Considering that DiMaggio played only 13 years and lost three prime season because of World War II, his 361 home runs are almost as impressive as Mantle's 536 DiMaggio was a better defensive center fielder than Mantle, which is not a put-down DiMaggio was a better center fielder than almost anyone else. DiMaggio struck ou less than Mantle — and almost everyone else — and as a result, he hit huge number of doubles and triples. He put a lot more balls in play than Mantle did.

The number of runs a team scores is essentially determined by how man runners it puts on base. Because he walked so often, Mantle was on base more tha DiMaggio was —a lot more. DiMaggio's on-base percentage was 44 points bette than the league norm; Mantle's was 92 points better. Mantle's walks won mor games for the Yankees than DiMaggio's defense — or at least than DiMaggio' defensive advantage.

Mantle had many other virtues as a player. His .801 career stolen-base percent-age is 15th-best all time. Mantle stole five times as many bases as DiMaggio did, and he grounded into considerably fewer double plays. Mantle could not sustain his speed like DiMaggio did, but he could run faster in a short burst than almost anyone.

Mantle was adored by millions of fans, but he never reached the acceptance that DiMaggio did with the cognoscenti—if it's not too absurd to refer to old sportswriters as cognoscenti. DiMaggio demanded, deserved, and received respect. Mantle adopted an "Aw Shucks" personality, never demanded respect in the same way and never received it. But he deserved it. He frequently played in pain, and he played magnificently.

JOE DiMAGGIO

"You have to grow up with baseball to play it well" — Babe Ruth said it and Joe)iMaggio illustrated the point. DiMaggio grew up in a time and place when serious base-ɔall was being played. His older brothers were ballplayers, and at the age of 18 DiMaggio ɔlayed 187 games in the Pacific Coast League, just one notch below the major leagues.

Unlike Mickey Mantle, who arrived in the najors as a raw package of formidable ability,)iMaggio knew how to play the game long before ıe first caught sight of the New York City skyline. ust weeks after his first game, DiMaggio had jaws gape all over the American League. The moment hey saw him, everyone in the baseball world real-zed that DiMaggio was very special.

DiMaggio was among a handful of players in ɔaseball history who did everything well. Swinging ı heavy bat, he drove long, arching line drives, and ıardly ever struck out. He ran not only fast but vith unparalleled grace, his strides melting one into another as he dashed over the vast, empty acres of center field at Yankee Stadium. He threw exceptionally well, and he played hard all the time.

A right-handed hitter in a park where the left field fence arched out to 400 feet before it reached center field, DiMaggio probably lost more home runs than any other player in history. He hit only 148 home runs in Yankee Stadium, and 213 on the road. He hit more road home runs than Mel Ott did, and in a much shorter career. Had he played half the time in just about any park except Yankee Stadium, DiMaggio likely would have hit 50 home runs in a good season.

For another player, Yankee Stadium's dimensions might have been a major detriment to his value. For DiMaggio, it simply emphasized other features of his game. If his long drives did not become home runs, they often became doubles or triples — and a showcase for his legendary grace. The huge left-center field area in Yankee Stadium was the perfect place for DiMaggio to display his fielding range.

After he retired, a myth grew that DiMaggio never made a baserunning error. This, of course, is silly; DiMaggio made many baserunning errors. The only people who never make mistakes are the people who never do anything. That myth started in the 1950s, when Willie Mays came along — arguably the only other "perfect" player in major league history. Mays stole bases, which DiMaggio did not, so some sportswriters of the day started the story that DiMaggio "never" made a mistake on the basepaths, trying to put him back on equal footing with Mays.

This assertion, while palpably false, is indicative of the effect DiMaggio had on those who saw him play. He came from hard times. He grew up poor, and he wasn't handsome or glib or witty. Baseball was what he had, a life raft. He learned to demand respect, and he learned dignity. He embodied dignity; he was dignity. It was one of DiMaggio's weapons — and he brought along every weapon he owned every time he went to the ballpark. The man did not like to lose.

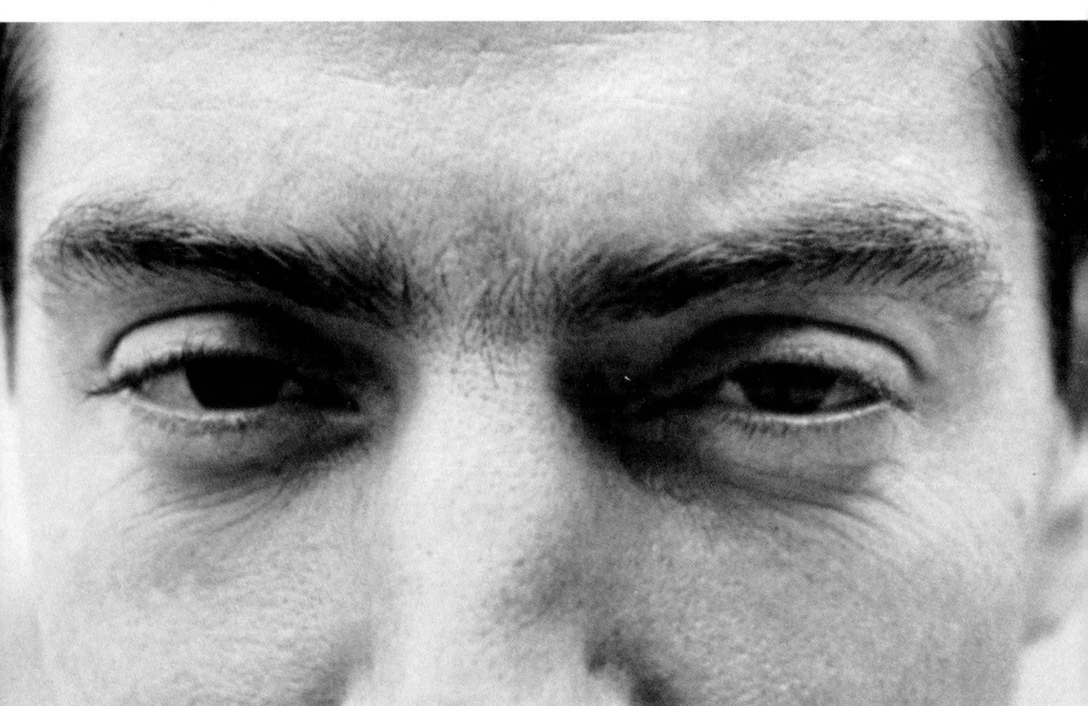

"There was nothing they could teach Joe D. When he came to the big leagues, IT WAS ALL THERE."

— JIMMY CANNON, New York sportswriter

DI.MAGGIO.5

Bernie Williams

During the 2002 American League Division Series, the television network broadcasting the games offered fans an opportunity to telephone in and cast their ballot for the Yankees' most valuable player. There were three choices, and Bernie Williams wasn't among them. He did get 204 hits, score 102 runs and drive in 102 runs. He was third in the league in hitting with a .333 average, and he did draw 83 walks, hit 37 doubles, and play center field in his usual stellar manner. But . . . Williams didn't do anything out of the ordinary for him, just what he had been doing every year.

Here is a trivia question: When was the last time that Ken Griffey Jr. out-hit Williams? Answer: 1994, when Griffey hit .323 and Williams .289.

The best way to understand why Williams was taken for granted is to remember what they taught you in the Army about camouflage. (If you were not in the Army, just follow along.) Anything that breaks up the silhouette of a person, they teach you in basic training, makes the person more difficult to see. The same concept applies to a ballplayer. If a player is accomplished in three, four, five areas, it is harder to recognize the breadth of his total accomplishment.

For about a decade, Williams spread his accomplishment all over the statistical map. He hit doubles and home runs, he drew walks, he hit for a high average, he ran well, he played a key defensive position and he batted from both sides of the plate. If you think about it, the following is not an outrageous statement: At the apex of his career, Williams did more things well than anyone else playing in the majors. He tended to be overlooked in discussions of the best players because his talent wasn't isolated in one area — it was everywhere.

The other thing you learn in the military about camouflage is that something moving attracts the eye. Let's apply that to baseball. If a player is good one year, great the next, fair the year after, great again two years later, that player tends to draw rave reviews because the media is taken by how well he plays when he plays well. Yet a player who is consistently good

year after year tends to fade into the scenery, just like the stationary object in our camouflage lesson. That was Bernie Williams — so steady and unwavering he went unnoticed.

Williams, who first wore Yankees pinstripes in 1991,was the cleanup hitter on four World Championship teams. Shoulder and knee injuries in 2002 and 2003 diminished his skills, but he remained a highly respected player.

In Yankees history through the 2004 All-Star Game, Williams ranked seventh in hits (the six ahead of him all are in the Hall of Fame), sixth in home runs, fifth in doubles, fifth in runs scored, ninth in RBIs, 12th in batting average (1,000 or more games), 10th in on-base percentage and ninth in games played. Yet few ever think to list him as one of the greatest Yankees. He plays the position that DiMaggio and Mantle played. Yes, DiMaggio and Mantle were better players than Williams, although Williams might finish with more hits than either of them.

Here is another perspective: Earle Combs, a fine Yankees outfielder in the 1920s and 1930s, clearly was not as good a player as Williams, yet Combs is in the Hall of Fame. Perhaps Williams will get there, too.

BEST OF THE REST

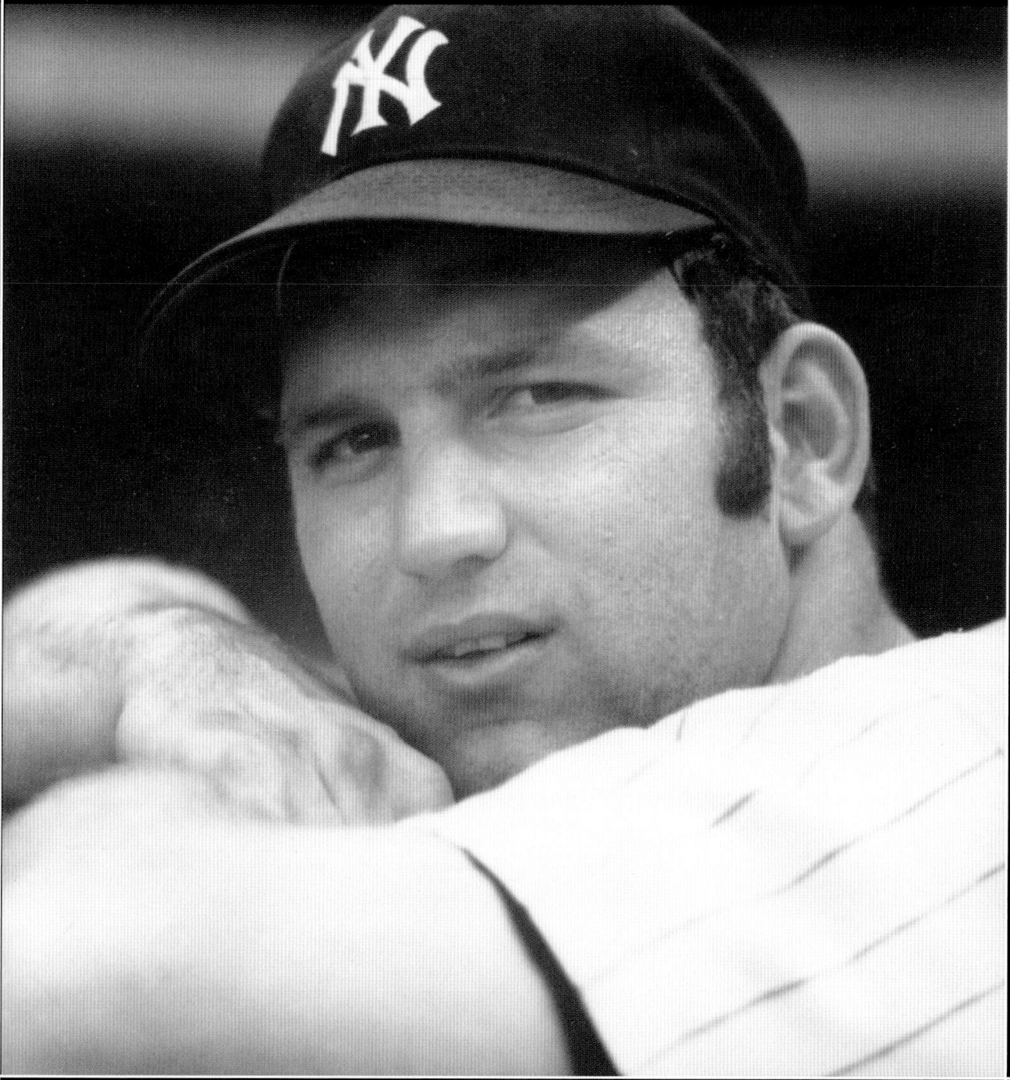

Best of the Rest

CATCHER

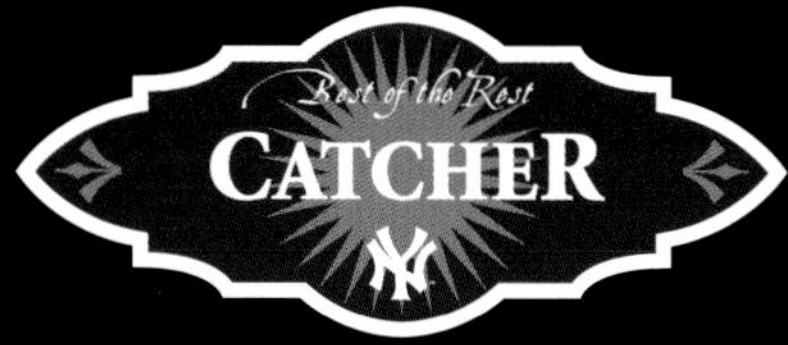

THURMAN MUNSON

Munson joined the Yankees during their lost years of the early 1970s and became an integral part of their revival. He was the American League MVP in 1976, when the Yankees made the World Series for the first time in 12 years. Munson was anything but a pretty player — a squat, grumpy-faced man usually in need of a shave. But he was the best catcher in the major leagues in his era not named Bench or Fisk, a hitter who produced runs with line-drive power and a receiver who had the respect of his pitchers and the other team's base-runners. Munson died in a plane crash in 1979, during his 11th season with the Yankees.

HIDEKI MATSUI

Long before he walked into Yankee Stadium, Matsui may as well have walked on water. He was among the most popular and respected players in the history of baseball in Japan, thanks to thundering power and an engaging personality and unassuming nature.

But beneath the polished exterior was a man preparing for the next challenge. Matsui couldn't resist the lure of the American majors, particularly when it meant joining the game's most storied franchise. In 2003 the Yankees landed Matsui to cover left field and break down the right-field wall.

The Yankees thought they were getting "Godzilla," as Matsui was known in his homeland, a feared and prodigious slugger who had blasted 322 home runs in nine seasons with the Yomiuri Giants, including 50 in 2002. Although Matsui hit only 16 home runs in his first season with the Yankees, he proved to be an exceptional player in virtually every facet of the game.

"We ended up with a better all-around player than we expected, despite not having the power bat he was built up to have," said Yankees general manager Brian Cashman. "He can beat you so many different ways. He can beat you with his glove, his bat, with little ball, with long ball. He can beat you with smart base running."

Matsui had 106 RBI, 42 doubles and a .291 batting average in 2003, remarkable achievements for someone adjusting to a foreign country and better pitching.

Matsui's power numbers rose significantly in the first half of 2004. By the All-Star break he had hit 18 home runs and was on pace for more than 30.

After a year and a half in America, Matsui had not missed a Yankees game and had played in two All-Star Games.

As Matsui's stature grew in the major leagues, his American admirers came to appreciate many of the same traits that made him a legend at home.

PAUL O'NEILL

For as long as hot-stove baseball is discussed, the Yankees' acquisition of Paul O'Neill for Roberto Kelly in 1993 will always be remembered as one of the all-time great moves of the snowy season.

In O'Neill, the Bombers landed a then-.259 lifetime hitter in six seasons with the Cincinnati Reds. During his Big Apple tenure, O'Neill soared far beyond all expectations, with a unique blend of timely hitting and defensive prowess along with an insatiable desire to succeed every time he stepped onto the field.

In nine seasons in pinstripes, O'Neill compiled a .303 batting average, which ranks 12th in franchise history. He won the 1994 American League batting title with a .359 average and was an American League All-Star four times.

In his first six seasons with the Yankees, O'Neill was the team's most consistent hitter, posting a .300-or-higher batting average in each of those campaigns while averaging 20 home runs per season during that span.

The career-.284 postseason hitter will forever be remembered as one of the cornerstones of the Yankees dynasty that won four World Series championships and five American League pennants between 1996 and 2001.

His statistics may have earned him a prominent spot in the Yankees record books, but it was his gritty play that earned him profound respect from his teammates and a permanent spot in the hearts of the Bronx faithful.

"He was just so competitive," Don Mattingly said. "His concentration was unbelievable. Day in and day out, he was ready to play. The way he played the game was amazing."

Yankees loyalists have seen a seemingly endless list of dramatic autumn moments in Yankee Stadium, and in O'Neill's last game in Ruth's House, they contributed to one that deserves a spot near the top of the list.

In the late hours of the Yankees' thrilling Game 5 win in the 2001 Fall Classic, 56,018 fans chanted the rightfielder's name for several minutes in chorus. At the conclusion of the inning, the humbled and emotional O'Neill tipped his cap to the adoring crowd, just before entering the home dugout.

Roger Clemens

Clemens joined the Yankees in 1999, at age 36, after 15 seasons and 233 victories with Boston and Toronto. The Rocket fashioned a 77-36 record in his five seasons with the Yankees, adding to his status as one of the greatest pitchers in major league history. Prior to 1999, Clemens had played in the World Series only once, as a member of the Red Sox team that lost to the New York Mets in 1986. He pitched in four World Series with the Yankees and earned two championship rings.

Clemens had a 3.99 earned-run average with the Yankees, completed three of his 157 starts and averaged 6⅓ innings per start. Those numbers paled in comparison to his first 15 seasons, when he had a 2.95 ERA, completed 114 of 449 starts and averaged 7⅓ innings per start. Yet he won at a greater rate with the Yankees (68.1 percent) than he had previously (65.3), a testament to his ability to pitch well despite diminishing physical skills and to the Yankees' extraordinary bullpen.

In 2001, Clemens became the first 20-game winner in history without a complete game; his 20-3 record merited him his sixth American League Cy Young Award.

On June 13, 2003, in his 20th major league season, the 40-year-old Clemens became the 21st pitcher to achieve 300 victories and the first to do it wearing the Yankees' pinstriped uniform. (Phil Niekro was the only other pitcher to win his 300th game while playing for the Yankees; he did it at Toronto, wearing the team's road gray uniform.) On that same June 13 night, in front of a sellout crowd of 55,214, Clemens also became the third pitcher in history to strike out 4,000 batters. He pitched 6⅔ innings and whiffed 10 in a 5-2 victory over the St. Louis Cardinals.

Clemens pitched for the Yankees for the final time in Game 4 of the 2003 World Series. After giving up three runs and five hits in the first inning, he stopped the Florida Marlins cold for the next six. With two outs in the seventh, Clemens struck out Luis Castillo. As he headed for the dugout, slapping his right hand into his glove, the crowd at Florida's Pro Player Stadium and all the men in both dugouts and bullpens stood in a rousing salute to Rocket, in his last game as a Yankee.

JORGE POSADA

Laugh if you want to, but there was a time not so long ago, February 2000 to be precise, when it was considered a risk by Yankees management to name Jorge Posada the full-time starting catcher. After all, Posada had seen limited action during the preceding three seasons as Joe Girardi's protégé during the Yanks' World Championships of 1996, 1998 and 1999.

"Posada will do just fine," promised legendary Yanks catcher Yogi Berra. "He has the tools, and he knows how to win. The rest takes care of itself."

Normally not prone to understatement, venerable Yogi was made a conservative forecaster after Posada proffered huge output for the Bombers in four full seasons since.

Not only were Posada's 100 home runs and 381 RBI tops among all American League catchers during that span, but the perennial All-Star backstop recently turned the weakest aspect of his game, calling pitches, into his strongest.

"Georgie has lived up to expectations and then some," said his skipper Joe Torre. "Without him, we don't have five trips to the World Series in six years."

In 2003, Posada nailed 26½ percent of prospective base thieves, placing him in baseball's Top 10 for the third consecutive season. Not to mention that Posada defended at such a high standard while simultaneously socking 30 homers with 101 RBI. He garnered third place in votes for '03 AL Most Valuable Player.

The popular Posada gradually has been gaining on hallowed team catching records of Berra, Bill Dickey, Elston Howard and Thurman Munson, but he also has taken aim at Yankee milestones for switch-hitters. While the numbers of Mickey Mantle, Bernie Williams and Roy White are safe for the time being, Posada's ability to connect from both sides of the plate only further diversifies the skills of a superlative Yankees weapon.

ROGER MARIS

Exclamation points punctuated various stages of Roger Maris' 12-year career. With four All-Star selections between 1959 and 1962, one Gold Glove Award in 1960, and the Most Valuable Player Award in 1960 and 1961, his talent seemed limitless. But his record-breaking accomplishments in 1961 temporarily branded him with baseball's Scarlet Letter—the asterisk.

In his second of six seasons with the Yankees, Maris broke Babe Ruth's single-season home run record of 60, set in 1927, on the final day of the 1961 season.

Maris was a quiet leader, unlike Ruth, who used his boisterous personality to curry fanfare. Ruth jested with the media where Maris shied from it. As the season progressed, it seemed like the public didn't want Ruth's record to be broken by an unassuming power hitter. The public felt that if Ruth's record were to fall, it had to be off the bat of a worthy goliath—someone like Mickey Mantle, who jockeyed for the home run lead with Maris that year. But the dinger-chase begat a mutually supportive friendship between the two teammates; the only feuds were conjured in newsrooms.

Maris was known more for being a team player who moved runners rather than knocking the ball into the stands. After 1961, Maris didn't hit more than 33 homers in a season and finished with a career total of 275.

When Maris hit the record-breaking shot on Oct. 1, 1961, some felt the record was tainted because Ruth did it in 151 games against the 161 it took Maris. For this reason, baseball commissioner Ford Frick placed an asterisk next to the accomplishment, in a way condemning him for the marvel that would stand another 37 years.

The asterisk was eventually removed, but 1961 remained the crest of Maris' career. That year, he also led the American League with 142 RBI and 132 runs scored en route to his second consecutive MVP Award and his first World Series title.

Rickey Henderson

Despite playing fewer than five full seasons with the Yankees, Rickey Henderson left a unique legacy of power and speed during his pinstriped tenure from 1985 through mid-1989. A 10-time All-Star, he is the Yankees' all-time leader in stolen bases with 326, and owns the top three single-season theft tallies in club history (93 in 1988, 87 in 1986, and 80 in 1985).

The Yankees acquired Henderson from the Oakland Athletics on Dec. 5, 1984, and the acquisition came with huge anticipation, as he already held three of the five highest single-season stolen base totals of the modern era, including the all-time record of 130 in 1982.

Often referred to simply as "Rickey," Henderson dazzled the Bronx faithful in 1985 by scoring a personal-best 146 runs in only 143 games. This feat was the highest Yankees single-season total since Joe DiMaggio's 151 in 1937. In 1986, Henderson established single-season highs with 28 homers (later tied in 1990) and 74 RBI.

Henderson stands in hallowed territory on many of baseball's all-time statistical charts, ranking first in runs scored (2,295), walks (2,190), and stolen bases (1,406). The future Hall of Famer won the American League Most Valuable Player Award in 1990 with the Athletics, and World Series rings with Oakland in 1989, and Toronto in 1993. A 12-time AL stolen base champion and five-time league leader in runs scored, Henderson became the 25th member of the 3,000-Hit Club (3,055 for career) in 2001.

GARY SHEFFIELD

Gary Sheffield hit 39 home runs, drove in 132 runs and scored 126 runs for the Atlanta Braves in 2003. The Yankees had not seen numbers like that from any of their outfielders, much less from the *same* outfielder, in almost 20 years.

To put Sheffield's brilliance in perspective, here is a listing of the last time a Yankees outfielder bettered Sheffield's 2003 numbers:

HOME RUNS	REGGIE JACKSON	41	1980
RBI	ROGER MARIS	142	1961
RUNS	RICKEY HENDERSON	146	1985

If his power numbers weren't enough, Sheffield batted .330 and had a .419 on-base percentage in 2003. In 32 years, only four Yankees outfielders had hit .330 (Bernie Williams, three times; Paul O'Neill; Dion James; and Dave Winfield), and only three had a higher on-base percentage (Williams, twice; O'Neill; and Rickey Henderson). With apologies to Williams, Jackson and Winfield, it can be argued that Sheffield, as a total offensive package, became the best Yankees outfielder since Mickey Mantle when he signed a three-year contract with the team in December 2003. At 35, Sheffield was still in his prime, a .300 hitter for six consecutive seasons, and one of 17 players in history who had achieved 300 home runs and 200 stolen bases for his career.

The Yankees were Sheffield's sixth team in his 17 major league seasons, a lot of uniform changes for a star of his magnitude. However, few players command as much respect from their peers, managers and coaches as Sheffield, does not only for his menacing bat, but also for his tough-minded approach to the game.

Orlando Hernandez

On June 3, 1998, Cuban righthander Orlando Hernandez took the mound in a spot-start for injured Yankees star David Cone on a few hours' notice. No matter that the enigmatic El Duque was just a few months removed from a death – defying defection raft ride to freedom in Anguilla Cay. The top *lanzador* helped beat Tampa 7-1, impressing his fans and critics alike with seven brilliant innings.

Under slightly less dramatic circumstances, Hernandez stepped up to the rubber again in early 2004 — also versus Tampa, also without having faced big-league level pitching in more than a year and also subbing for an ailing top starter (this time Mike Mussina). The result wasn't much different, as El Duque and the Yanks dumped the D-Rays, 10-3, after Duque threw 55 of 88 pitches for strikes.

"This is exactly what I was looking forward to," said Hernandez through a translator, "getting back to see all of my teammates and the great fans here"

By "getting back," El Duque was referring to the 20-month hiatus he took from his Yanks career, partially as a result of a trade to the Montreal Expos after the '02 campaign and partially a result of shoulder problems vexing him since his earliest days as a pro.

"Duque is in our plans…" said Yanks manager Joe Torre. "He still needs to get arm strength back, but he hasn't forgotten how to pitch."

Hernandez posted a 53-38 record during his five-year original stint with the Yanks, including a career-best 17-9 in 1999. But Duque has been better known for his postseason exploits. One of the top playoff pitchers in history, Hernandez is 9-3 lifetime, with a 2.51 ERA, in October. His dominating ALCS against Oakland in '99 won him the MVP trophy for that series.

Charlie Keller

"King Kong," as Charles Ernest Keller was better known — more as a result of his muscular physique and hirsute appearance than for disorderly behavior — served as stalwart outfielder of the wartime Yanks for six pennant-winning squads and four world titleists.

After a monster career in the minors — the apex being Keller named 1937 Minor League Player of the Year by *The Sporting News* — Kong had trouble finding a place in the bigs.

His patience was rewarded in '39, when the Yanks made room for the 22-year-old in the Bronx. The outfielder paid the Pinstripers fast dividends: a .334 rookie season with 83 RBI, on one of the best teams in baseball history, no less.

The five-time All-Star recorded 33 home runs and 122 RBI in his best year (1941) and averaged 27 homers per season over a seven-year span ('41–46) in spite of interruption for World War II military duty.

With a .306 lifetime World Series average as a testament to Keller's productivity in the clutch, he was a favorite of teammates and fans alike. King Kong's career was cut short by a congenital back disease, which retired him to the family farm in Maryland in his early 30s.

SPUD CHANDLER

Spud Chandler was a winner. The Yankees righthander owned the best winning percentage (.717) for pitchers with 100 or more victories when he retired in 1947 with the record of 109-43.

The baseball and football star at the University of Georgia first put on pinstripes in 1937 at the age of 29. In 1943, Chandler led the league in wins with a 20-4 record in 253 innings. His 1.64 ERA was another league-best, as were his 20 complete games and five shutouts. Since the Cy Young Award didn't yet exist, that performance earned him the league's Most Valuable Player Award.

He furthered his reputation as a big-game pitcher in the 1943 postseason, earning two World Series wins, including the clincher. In six career World Series games, Chandler was 2-2 with a 1.62 ERA.

HERB PENNOCK

Lefthanded pitcher Herb Pennock starred on the dominant Yankees teams of the 1920s and early 1930s that won five American League championships and four World Series. Relying on an encyclopedic knowledge of opposing hitters, Pennock issued few walks and forced hitters to put the ball in play.

Pennock was acquired from the Boston Red Sox in January 1923. In his inaugural campaign in pinstripes, he went 19-6 while leading the American League in winning percentage (.760). He then paced the Yankees in wins the following three years with 21 in 1924, 16 in 1925, and 23 in 1926.

Pennock finished his career with a 240-162 record and 3.60 ERA, going 5-0 in World Series play. He was inducted into the Hall of Fame in 1948.

Jason Giambi

While many players would have found it intimidating to replace fan favorite Tino Martinez at first base in the Bronx, as Jason Giambi did in signing with the Yankees as a free agent in 2001, Giambi at least had some training in the matter.

When the Oakland A's traded home run colossus Mark McGwire to the St. Louis Cardinals in 1997, Giambi didn't miss a beat in taking over at first for Mac — he improved his offensive numbers in three successive seasons, culminating in a 43-homer, 137-RBI campaign in 2000 to win the A.L. Most Valuable Player Award.

"The Giambino," as he is affectionately known by broadcasters, recorded 82 home runs in his first two years in pinstripes. Giambi boasts a lifetime .407 on-base percentage, an amazing feat considering the slugger averages more than 100 strikeouts per season.

Mike Mussina

Mussina joined the Yankees in 2001, after a decade with the Baltimore Orioles, for whom he was one of the most reliable pitchers in the major leagues. Mussina had an exceptional first season with the Yankees, winning 17 games and posting a 3.15 ERA that ranked second in the American League. He was not as consistent in 2002, when his ERA rose by nearly a run, although he won 18 games. In 2003 Mussina finished with a 3.40 ERA and had 17 wins.

Mussina is among the elite class of pitchers who can rely on both power and control. He throws a fastball in the 90-mph range, and his knuckle-curveball has long been recognized as one of the hardest pitches to hit in the major leagues. Mussina can throw five pitches with uncanny control, leaving hitters off-balance. Not surprisingly, he has taken a no-hitter into the eighth inning on four occasions — including a nailbiter against Boston in 2001. Mussina is an exceptional athlete, having won six Gold Gloves for his fielding.

Bobby Murcer

From Earle Combs to Joe DiMaggio to Mickey Mantle, the man in center field for the Yankees was destined for the Hall of Fame. Murcer was next in that link, and he turned out to be merely a very good player. He was a solid No. 3 hitter in the lineup and a reliable center fielder. The media never gave Murcer his due, largely because the Yankees were also-rans most of the time he was with them; the best players on a bad team usually get the most blame. By the time the Yankees started winning again, Murcer had been traded to San Francisco. He came back to the Yankees in 1979 and completed his career as a part-time player. In 1983, Murcer returned to the team as a broadcaster.

Wally Pipp

Pipp is most famous for losing his job to Lou Gehrig, but he was a good player in his own right, comparable to someone like Bill Buckner or Chris Chambliss in the 1970s and 1980s. Pipp, the Yankees' regular first baseman for 10 years, twice led the American League in home runs and had a four-year run in which he drove in from 90 to 114 runs. Pipp played defense better than any first baseman in the major leagues except for another man in his town, George Kelly of the Giants.

Mel Stottlemyre

The Yankees were in third place when Stottlemyre joined the team in August 1964. He won nine games in six weeks, leading the Yankees to the pennant, the only time the team made the World Series in his 11 seasons. Stottlemyre won 20 games in three of the next five seasons, despite the degeneration of the team around him. He started at least 35 games for nine consecutive seasons, a feat matched in the 20th Century only by Gaylord Perry, who did it 10 times. Elston Howard said Stottlemyre threw the best slider he ever saw. Stottlemyre's sinker was equally famous, and he was adept at changing speeds on all of his pitches. Stottlemyre became the Yankees pitching coach in 1995.

Dave Righetti

Righetti was a successful starter for the Yankees for three years, going 33-22, including an Independence Day no-hitter against Boston in 1983. When the team needed a replacement for closer Goose Gossage in 1984, Righetti accepted the assignment and flourished in the role for seven years, averaging more than 30 saves. He had 46 saves in 1986, a major league record until 1990. When he went to the bullpen, Righetti was able to pare his repertoire to his two above-average pitches, a lively fastball and a hard-bending curve. Righetti is the Yankees all-time leader in appearances by a pitcher with 522.

Catfish Hunter

Hunter had most of his best years with the Oakland Athletics, but in 1975 he justified George Steinbrenner's free-agent investment in him by having one of the best seasons ever by a Yankees pitcher. Hunter's 328-innings season that year — his first of five with the Yankees — was exceeded in the rest of the century only by Phil Niekro, who did it three times. Hunter made 75 starts over the 1975 and 1976 seasons, a two-year total that was surpassed only once — again by Niekro — in the final quarter of the 20th Century. Hunter's 30 complete games in 1975 has not been topped, largely because no *team* has had that many since 1989.

Andy Pettitte

The gangly Texan in just one decade in pinstripes, made a compelling case for being the second-best lefty in Yankees history. Pettitte entered 2004 with a superb career record of 149-78. Whitey Ford, for comparison's sake, at that age was 105-40, and Ron Guidry was 76-29. Ford pitched for nine more seasons, winning another 131 games before retiring. Guidry had 94 victories after turning 30. Durable and reliable for most of his career, Pettitte averaged 31 starts per year until 2002, when injuries limited him to 22 starts.

Sparky Lyle

In an era of trumped-up offense, it's almost incomprehensible how a pitcher could retain a sub-3.00 lifetime ERA, especially over the course of 16 seasons. But things were different 30 years ago, and Sparky Lyle was at the nexus of it all, with a 2.88 ERA while accumulating three All-Star selections in 1973, 1976, and 1977. At the age of 32, Lyle won the Cy Young Award in 1977. All this without ever starting a game.

Lyle changed how relievers were regarded in his heyday with effective sliders, curveballs, and fastballs. He led the league in saves in 1972 with 35. In 1977, Lyle won 13 games with a 2.17 ERA and 26 saves in 137 innings pitched.

In franchise history, the lefthander ranks sixth all-time in appearances (420), and fourth in saves (141).

Bob Meusel

Blessed with a powerful throwing arm from the outfield, Bob Meusel compiled a .309 career batting average while playing 10 of 11 major league seasons with the powerhouse Yankees clubs of the 1920s.

Often overshadowed in pinstripes, Meusel is 10th on the Bombers all-time RBI list with 1,005. He was an excellent all-around player, having led the Yankees five times in stolen bases between 1921 and 1927. He also stands at seventh place in Yankees history in triples with 87, and eighth in career doubles with 338.

Meusel's best season was 1925, as he led the American League with 33 homers, 138 RBI, and 79 extra-base hits. But he was consistently productive throughout the decade, knocking in more than 100 runs five times, scoring more than 100 runs twice, while being a member of three Yankees World Series teams in 1923, 1927 and 1928.

EARLE COMBS

Earle Combs only needed 12 seasons in the Bronx before his ticket was punched for Cooperstown. And with a nickname like "The Kentucky Colonel," what else would be expected?

Wearing only Yankees pinstripes between 1924 and 1935, it's no surprise that the centerfielder ranks in the Top 20 in seven franchise categories, including four in the Top 10. Among them, Combs ranks 11th in doubles (309), ninth in hits (1,866), sixth in runs (1,186), third in average (.325) and second in triples (154).

As a part the 1927 Murderers' Row Yanks, arguably the toughest lineup ever, Combs led the league in hits (231) and triples (23). He was on three World Series winners in 1927, 1928 and 1932. Combs was inducted into the Hall of Fame in 1970.

TOMMY JOHN

After compiling 171 wins in his first 14 major league seasons, Tommy John burst onto the Bronx scene in 1979. He didn't waste much time in carving his name into Yankees lore, as he posted a 21-9 record with a 2.96 ERA along with three shutouts and a career-best 17 complete games.

As an encore to his sensational debut season in New York, John surpassed his career-high in wins in 1980 with a 22-9 record. During that campaign, he added 16 more complete games and a league-leading six shutouts to his résumé.

John was at his best when it mattered most. In two World Series appearances (five starts), he posted a 2.67 ERA, allowing only ten runs in 33⅔ innings of work.

The career 288-game winner was traded to California during the 1982 season but eventually returned to the Yankees in 1986. In his final four seasons, John won 29 games for the Pinstripers.

GEORGE SELKIRK

Although most Canadian youths hone their skills on the ice, George Selkirk chose to pursue baseball during his Ontario upbringing. Selkirk got his first call-up after an eight-year minor-league career. With the promotion came the pressure of replacing Babe Ruth in right field. Selkirk also inherited the Bambino's No. 3.

The pressure didn't faze Selkirk, as he batted .312 in his debut season of 1934. From that point on, his star continued to rise, as he batted more than .300 in four of the next five seasons, topping off at .328 in 1937.

In 1936, he played in his first World Series, a six-game Yankees triumph over their crosstown rival New York Giants. In that Fall Classic, Selkirk posted a .333 average with two homers.

The two-time All-Star recorded a .290 lifetime average and went on to play in five more World Series, amid one of the greatest Yankees dynasties, in which the Pinstripers won five championships in six years (1936–1941).

WAITE HOYT

Waite Hoyt anchored the pitching staff of great Yankees teams of the 1920s. Nicknamed "Schoolboy" after being initially signed at age 15 by the rival New York Giants, Hoyt saved his best for the World Series. Pitching for the Yankees against the Giants in the 1921 Series, Hoyt tossed three complete games without allowing an earned run. In seven Series (six with the Yankees), he was 6-4 with a 1.83 ERA over 83⅔ innings pitched.

Hoyt led the American League in wins (22) and earned run average (2.63) behind the colossal lineup of the 1927 Murderers' Row Yanks. On the 1928 championship club, he compiled a 23-7 record with a league-leading eight saves.

Elected to the Hall of Fame in 1969, Hoyt finished with a career 237-182 record (157-98 for the Yankees) and a 3.59 ERA.